NETHERTON

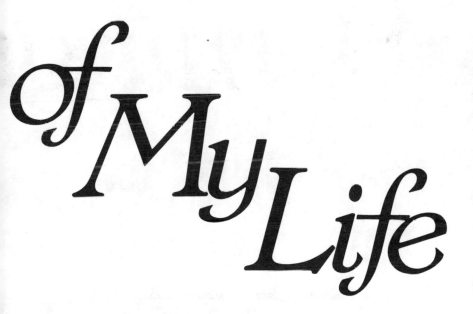

of My Life

TYNDALE HOUSE
PUBLISHERS, INC.
WHEATON, ILLINOIS

17 38

Foreword by Norma Zimmer

I was elated when Tom Netherton asked me to write a foreword to his book. It's a pleasure for me to share my admiration for this tall, handsome baritone with the magnificent, God-given voice. I have found Tom to be one of the most sincere, loving, and compassionate young men I have ever met.

Through the years that we have worked together, both on the Lawrence Welk Show and in personal appearances, Tom has always been a complete professional. He loves his audiences, and is always fully prepared to share the love of God through word and song. I wish you all could see Tom behind the scenes. He has a wonderful sense of humor—yes, a genuine sense of fun that keeps everyone in high spirits.

I'm thrilled that now you will get to know this young man better through his absorbing story. Like most of us, Tom has experienced discouragement and uncertainty, but through his unwavering faith, he has surmounted his problems. You'll learn that Tom has a very real personal relationship with his Savior. He also has a rare ability to share the love, the truth, and the power of Jesus Christ.

I commend *In the Morning of My Life* to you, whether you are married or single, young or old, male or female. What Tom has to say will speak to the heart and need of every reader.

Foreword
by Lawrence
Welk

So many times throughout my life, I've realized anew how much I owe my many friends! That's especially true of my dear friends Sheila and Harold Schafer, of North Dakota. They're the ones who "found" Tom Netherton for me, and—as Tom explains so nicely in this book—arranged things so I could hear him sing, when I was home visiting my family and friends in North Dakota.

Tom sang for me one afternoon, after a round of golf at the Apple Creek Country Club in Bismarck, and the moment I heard him, I felt he would be just right for our show. In the five years since that time, he has more than justified my faith in him. His exceptional baritone voice has been of tremendous help in brightening up our show—and his six-foot-five-inches of Danish good looks haven't hurt either! Tom has become one of our "biggest" stars, in more ways than one, and is in constant demand to make personal appearances all over the nation. All this makes me very happy, and proud of him.

But I am perhaps even more proud of Tom as a person than as a performer, because he has tried, through all the years I've known him, to live according to God's Laws. I've been around a bit longer than he, so I know from long experience that it's the only way to live, and—as I've explained in some of my own books—I've been grateful all my life that my parents gave me the gift of faith at birth. They started me out on the right road, and it makes me deeply happy that Tom has found and tries to stay on that road too.

It's a great personal pleasure for me to welcome this fine and dedicated young man into the literary world, and I wish him every success, not only with his book—but with his life.

*In the
Morning
of My
Life*

Chapter One

He wears a black velvet dinner jacket trimmed in sparkling black sequins and glass beading. Underneath is a black jumpsuit trimmed in sequins. He is smiling, poised, and perfectly at home on the small supper club stage. The sound of the full orchestra behind him is exhilarating as it plays the overture for his new act, and the dynamics of the moment are electric. The crowd senses it.

"Ladies and gentlemen, the Blue Room at the Fairmont is proud to present—Mr. Tom Netherton!"

He is singing now and the audience is applauding; someone whistles. Sitting ringside is an older woman—could be his mother, and beside her another older woman—could be his grandmother. At a nearby table is a group of young people. They look like the young people he went to school with back in Minnesota. Somehow the entire audience looks familiar to him. They could be aunts, uncles, cousins, old friends. But that's how he usually feels about his audiences. He likes to look at them as friends.

He sings to a young girl in a yellow dress at a front table, *"You stepped out of a dream. . ."* She blushes uncontrollably. The audience loves it.

He listens for the piano and smiles at the girl. *". . . you are too wonderful to be what you seem. . . ."* Somewhere in the back of his mind he hears the voice of his younger brother, Brad. He remembers the dining room of his mother's house. Brad is standing there in the doorway, his mouth hanging open.

"What? My brother, Tom, is going to be in a musical? You mean he can *sing?*"

The young girl in the yellow dress trembles and blushes a deeper crimson, like so many others he sings to in the audiences. He smiles, enjoying the pictures flashing through his thoughts.

"Could there be eyes like yours? . . ."

"Yes, Brad. It looks like I'm going to sing in a musical."

"You?"

"That's right. They picked me to sing the lead."

"I know you can run and you sure can swim—but I didn't know you could *sing!*"

"Neither did I, Brad. Believe me, neither did I."

"Could there be smiles like yours?"

After the show the people line up in the shadows of the tables along the aisles of blue carpeting and wait for his autograph. They ask to take his picture with Aunt Maude or beside Sister Sue or Cousin Millie. He smiles and writes, *God bless,*

Tom Netherton on their menus, autograph books, napkins, matchbooks, bits of paper.

Then they are all gone. The musicians go home. The waiters and busboys clear away the blue tablecloths, the blue candles, the blue menus, and they vacuum the blue carpeting. He leaves through the door in the kitchen, takes the back elevator up to his suite on the eighteenth floor. He is alone.

But not entirely. Brad's voice still buzzes in his mind. He remembers the smell of his mother's beef stew coming from the kitchen. The table in the dining room is set with plates and knives and forks, ready for the evening meal. His brother tosses his football helmet on a chair.

"Come on, you're kidding. You're not really going to *sing*, are you?"

"Yes. I really am going to sing."

"You got the *lead?* I mean, the *lead?*"

"Right. I got the lead."

His younger sister passes with a plate of biscuits.

"Come on, you guys. Sit down. We're going to eat now."

"How come?"

"Because dinner's ready."

"No, I mean, how come *you* got the lead?"

"I don't know. I just did."

They sit at the table, a family of six evenly distributed, with father at one end, mother at the other, and two children at each side. There are two boys and two girls, a neat package, and no mother could be more proud of her family than Lillian Netherton. She bubbles with enthusiasm now. "Tell us *all* about it, Tom."

"Tell about what?"

"About the musical!"

"Well, I was dared to audition so I did. Julie, will you pass the butter? We were returning from track practice. No, not the salt, the butter. And then today at school I saw the cast list posted—"

Brad interrupts. "And there's his name: TOM NETHERTON dash dash, the lead! Can you imagine? And I never heard him sing around here once, not even in the shower!"

"Well, the school is the biggest high school in Minnesota," Mom says. "Tom, will you pass Wendy the salad? Now, Wendy, take some salad. I mean, they can't be that hard up for decent voices at that school."

What happened was, I had gone to watch the Senior Musical auditions with another friend of mine and we sat in the back row laughing and making fun of everybody else who was auditioning. It was a stupid thing to do but we thought it would be a lot of fun. We had just walked into the choir room after track practice and sat down in the seats in the back, that's all. We weren't even making any noise yet.

But then one of my friends dared me to audition. We all laughed as though it was the biggest joke in the world. Actually, to me it was. So then I dared my friend.

He took up my dare and said, "OK, I'll do it if you will."

I told him, "It's a deal."

He went up on stage and made a real fool of

himself. We laughed so hard we were nearly in tears. Then it was my turn.

There were at least two hundred kids there, maybe more. I suddenly regretted taking up the dare. I was humiliated right down to my feet. Well, I got up there and started singing a song I knew, "Almost Like Being in Love." The musical they were going to do was Brigadoon.

I looked down as I was singing and there was a girl in the front row crying. She was actually in tears! I thought, "I must be so bad that this girl is weeping in pity for me." It was a terrible experience. I don't know how I got through it.

Then I finished the song and all of a sudden everyone in the whole place was cheering, yelling, applauding, and just plain going bananas. I was sure they were making fun of me. I put the music down, walked up the aisle to the seat where I had left my books, and stalked out.

I was totally humiliated.

The telephone is ringing as he enters his suite on the eighteenth floor. Actually about five of them ring; there is a telephone on nearly every flat surface.

"Hello?"

"Hello, Tom!"

It is his agent.

"Can you be back in L.A. on the sixteenth?"

"Well, it'll take some shuffling. I've got the concert at Lee High Acres after I close here in New Orleans, and then I go to Nashville for another recording session—"

"We'd better do the shuffling, Tom. They want you for the 'Jim Nabors Show.' "

"Great!"

"And 'The Dating Game'—"

"Terrific."

"And, just for your interest, your concert date at the Van Wezel in Sarasota is almost sold out. Advance ticket sales are going great."

"Beautiful."

"Not bad, eh?"

"No, not bad."

Sinking into the gold and blue satin sofa against the blue flocked wall of his opulent suite at the Fairmont Hotel, he smiles and waves a silent tribute to *Brigadoon* and a dare that more or less started it all.

Chapter Two

I was a baby when *Brigadoon* was first produced on Broadway. In fact, it opened the year I was born—1947. My father was a captain in the 504th Infantry Division at the time, stationed in Europe. I was born in Munich, Germany, at the Ninety-eighth General Hospital.

The war was over, the depression past, the economy on the rise, and American occupation troops returning home. I was nine months old when I had my first encounter with the press. A photographer at the *New York Daily Mirror* took a picture of returning occupation families and snapped one of my mother and me through the porthole of the transport *Alexander*. My mother was all smiles, waving happily with one arm and holding me with the other. She had me dressed in a white suit with a white beret perched on the side of my head. (I was as round as a Danish dumpling.)

The next day our picture was on every news-stand across the country with a caption reading, "First sight of his homeland evokes wide-eyed wonder in little Tommy Netherton."

We were on our way to Fort Bragg, North Carolina, where my father had orders to join the Eighty-second Airborne Division.

Our home was a converted wooden barracks painted white with wooden steps leading up to it. On the top step was a white identification strip you could see from the road: CAPT. T. H. NETHERTON. Every day I could watch the army trucks and jeeps stream past along the dirt road by our house.

It was a barren, drab, and sandy place. I didn't mind the sand in the yard, because I played for hours in it, carving out roads and forts for my own toy tanks and trucks to forge across. In the house it was another story because there was always sand under my feet, in the cushions of the furniture, and even in the beds. If it was a particularly windy day, the wind would blow the sand in under the door.

In 1950, the year the Korean War broke out, my brother Brad was born. I was three years old. I was glad when I heard my mother had a boy because I figured I'd have a new playmate, but I hadn't counted on his being quite so small.

We said good-bye to our little wooden house at Fort Bragg when my father was transferred to another army post at Fort Benning, Georgia. It was here I was to face one of the first hurdles of life—attending kindergarten.

I was not at all enthusiastic about the idea of

Left: I was nine months old when I first came to America.
Right: This picture of Mom and me was taken in Munich,
Germany, where I was born.

FIRST SIGHT of his homeland evokes wide-eyed
wonder in little Tommy Netherton, as mother Lillian
shows him New York. Born in Munich, where his
Army-captain dad was stationed, Tommy arrived
here yesterday on transport Alexander.

Left: Front page news! The New York Daily Mirror *carried this
photo of Mom and me arriving in the U.S. from Europe.
Right: With Mom and Dad at Ft. Bragg, N.C., January
1950.*

getting out on my own into such an ominous and frightening world as kindergarten. One day we drove past the school. "See, Tom?" my mother encouraged. "Look at all the nice children playing in the schoolyard. You'll have such a nice time here. Look, Tom. See, they're playing ball! Isn't that nice? Wouldn't you like to do that, too?"

That did it. "I'm not going to kindergarten. I'm not going." You see, when I saw those children playing ball, I realized I didn't know how to play ball, or to participate in any of their sports. I didn't know how to run bases or hit a ball or toss a ball and I had no idea how to catch one. I felt miserably self-conscious and begged my mother not to send me there.

I overcame the kindergarten trauma although I never did attend. I worked every day at trying to figure out how to play baseball. I thought if I could get it down by the time I had to go to first grade, I'd be all right.

I had another Welcome-to-Fort-Benning experience I could have done without when one of the boys threw a tin can at my head and sliced a hunk out of my face right beneath my eye. My mother, panic-stricken, rushed me, bloodsoaked and stunned, to the doctor's office. "Just pray it will heal," he told her. "We can't stitch it up. It's too close to the eye." I left the office with a white gauze patch across my face.

Two weeks later I was outside playing with my ball and the same boy who had thrown the can at me the first time threw a piece of black, sooty coal at me. This time the jagged edge chopped me right beneath the other eye. My mother rushed me off again, bleeding and bewildered, to the same doctor. He shook his head in amazement.

"It's a good thing you've got only two eyes. If you had more, I'd run out of patches." But then he said the wound had almost severed the nerve. Again he couldn't stitch, just patch. I was some sight—patched, swollen, and scabbed. Happily, I healed well though the scars took years to go away.

In the summer of 1953 my sister Julie was born. She was barely three months old when my father received orders for Korea. That meant we would be moving again.

Now I began to experience a typical malady of service life; it had to do with making and keeping friends. The people on the post were there for different lengths of time, so you could make friends one day and the next they'd be assigned to a different post or sent overseas. For a child it could be lonely.

It was for me.

It was a sad experience when I watched one of my friends moving to another place. I stood in the sand with the wind and dust blowing all around, watching the family climb into the car. They started off and I ran after the car, waving. I could see my friend's face pressed against the back window. We were both crying and waving at each other. Then they were gone and I was alone.

But after awhile you stop crying. You just accept it. I figured friends were not for keeps.

Chapter
Three

The radio was playing "Don't Fence Me In" in the other room as my father picked up his duffle bag and swung it over his shoulder. He was enormous, really enormous. To us children he was like a giant—6' 5" tall, broad shouldered, and when he spoke it was with a deep, bass voice. Just the sound of him moving around in the house kept us at attention.

He was leaving for Korea, assigned as Provost Marshal of the Second Infantry Division. "I'll be gone for a long, long time," he told Brad and me. We didn't know exactly what that meant.

It was decided that we would move to Chicago, Illinois, to live with my mother's parents. That way there would be someone to look after my mother and us children while Father was gone.

The idea of moving in with my grandparents was a happy one. My grandparents were the dearest people on earth; in fact, we kids loved them so much we called them Mom and Dad.

We arrived at their house in Chicago and said good-bye to my father. Our boxes were still packed and standing in piles in Grandpa's garage, our furniture stacked in one corner next to the rakes, the spades, and the lawn mower. Then my father left.

The wind blew some leaves around on the sidewalk outside and I sat in the big overstuffed armchair in my grandparents' living room and watched Ed Sullivan and the dancing Toastettes on television.

My grandparents were both born in Denmark and their cozy bungalow at 79th and Harvard held colorful memorabilia of their old country. There was always a Danish calendar hanging on the wall in the kitchen with a color picture of Copenhagen, and in the living room were stacks of Danish newspapers which only my grandfather read. On the walls there were yellowed pictures of my mom and her sisters when they were babies, and African violets sat in bunches on tables in the dining room. It always smelled of something baking in the oven, and the hallway leading to the bedrooms held the faint smell of pomander balls.

My grandfather was a balding man with sloping shoulders, a long face, wide nose, and an upturned smile that was happier than any circus. His smile was better than a free gift from the ice cream man. Sometimes that smile, if it had a certain playful twinkle, meant Come-on-run-as-fast-as-you-can-toward-me-and-I'll-catch-you, and so I would come a-running, and jump into his strong arms and hug him with all my might. Sometimes he'd toss me into the air and catch me in mid-flight as I squealed with laughter.

He was a cement contractor and when he'd come home from work in the evening I'd run down the sidewalk to meet him. I'd reach for his black lunch pail and then, walking proud and tall, I'd carry the lunch pail to the house while talking happily and laughing with him.

On Saturday afternoons Grandpa would put polka records on the phonograph part of the combination television-radio-phonograph that lined one wall of the living room, and he'd dance with my mom or my grandmother. Then he'd hold baby Julie in his arms and twirl around the room with her, singing, "Tralala twiddly dee dee, it gives me a t'rill. . . ." I would sit on the green flowered sofa clapping and singing along. When he played "Whoopie John" or one of his Danish records, I was barely able to sit still.

He taught me how to step-hop-step-hop turn-around, step-hop, that's it, keep a-going, you've got it dere, step-hop—and I'd be the star of the show as he laughed and applauded my efforts.

Downstairs in the basement was Grandpa's mysterious "workshop," where I was sure there were monsters hungrily lurking. There beneath the house were the things that made grandpas special people.

Things like his tools and workbench and calendars that Grandma wouldn't allow in the kitchen. He had an old Halloween skeleton hanging on the door and that made it a foreboding and forbidden place for me. I'd peek down into the darkness, the

With Dad and grandparents. I proudly wore an army uniform just like my dad's.

damp, dark smells drifting upward, and I'd decide to do my carpentry upstairs, possibly on the lawn.

The months passed quickly and eating Grandma's homemade Danish coffee cake and meatballs ended, as well as dancing to the strains of "The Tennessee Waltz" and "The Mocking Bird Song." We moved into our own house in Palos Heights, a suburb of Chicago.

It was nice having our own house but I missed my grandparents, especially my grandpa. Nearly every day I asked my mom, "When can we go over to Grandpa's?" The large oak trees shaded our little house, and listening to the wind blowing at night in the leaves, I would imagine I was Flash Gordon and my rocket ship awaited me in the shadows of the backyard. I'd fly in it to Grandma and Grandpa's and he would be, as he always was, happy to see me.

"Ah! It's my little feller!" he'd shout from the door. He'd stretch out his arms to me and I'd run as fast as I could toward him—toward my grandpa who loved me.

The radio was on in the kitchen and I heard Percy Faith's "Song from Moulin Rouge." I frowned and clipped the stiff little bow tie to my collar. My first day of school was here. My pencils and notebook were neatly tucked into my book bag. I ate my Wheaties, Breakfast of Champions, climbed into our Oldsmobile with my mom, and unhappily arrived at the brick building fifteen minutes before the bell rang.

On that first day I stood in front of a little wooden flower box filled with spindly flowers to have my picture taken. I wore my school bag strapped across my chest and smiled a big toothy smile even though I was scared. I dragged my feet, wearing new shoes with thick rubber soles, as I walked across the grass to the low brick building to face the dreaded experience ahead. I entered my classroom and took one look at my stern-faced teacher and knew for certain I wasn't going to like first grade.

Second grade was a little better; it was, in fact, a momentous year for me. On the first day of school I walked into my room and got my first glimpse of my new teacher. It was love at first sight. Her name was Miss Adams and she smiled a friendly smile when we were introduced. She welcomed me to the class, and later, as I watched her standing before us, her cheeks flushed and her eyes dancing, I felt instantly at home. My mom never had to force me to go to school as long as Miss Adams was my teacher.

During my first few years in school I often visited my grandparents. On one visit I remember sitting in the kitchen looking out the window at the ragman as he vanished down the alley. The clop-clop of his homely horse, the creaking of the old wagon, and the whining ragman call ("Raaaags! Ol' iron!") had become familiar sounds to me.

Suddenly I saw Grandpa enter the yard with some of his old men friends. They were going to play horseshoes. Just the sight of him made me feel happy. I watched as he reached back and tossed the horseshoe through the air, low along the ground. The other men, standing in the shade of the trees smoking cigars and talking, had a sort of ease and slowness about them. It seemed whatever they were doing, they always had time for a young child.

"Dad!" I called.

"Ah!" he called back, "it's my little feller!"

I'd stay with him all afternoon as the old men played horseshoes, smoked their cigars, and discussed the Detroit Lions defeating the Cleveland Browns and John Foster Dulles shaping up the foreign policy and Eisenhower's merits as President.

"Think he'll do a better job than Truman?"

"Of course. He's a Republican, isn't he?"

"We'll have to forgive him for that."

Sometimes they'd argue, but their words were always gentle, slow, as though having someone to talk to was more important than being right or wrong.

At night, sitting cross-legged on the maroon flowered rug in the living room, I'd put together the big wooden puzzle of the United States. Sometimes my grandpa would play Monopoly with me and sometimes he'd tell me stories about when he was a boy in Denmark, and I'd be completely happy.

Chapter Four

By now I was perhaps one of the most experienced cowboys in all of Palos Heights. I was so good at being a cowboy, I think I could have out-Roy Rogered Roy Rogers. I had a cowboy wardrobe complete with six-shooters, sweat bands, hats, shirts, vests, leather cuffs and chaps, and of course, the fanciest boots this side of the Mississippi.

Miss Adams frowned on my bringing my wild west regalia to school, but after I practiced for eleven days, she was impressed when I twirled my six-shooters for Tuesday's Show-and-Tell.

I chewed Wrigley's Spearmint Gum along with Gene Autrey while humming "I'm back in the saddle again, out where a friend is a friend." I often came home for dinner, flung open the door, guns drawn, and shouted in a dreadful voice, "It's me, Ceeeesco!" Mom would smile, "Wash your hands, Cisco Kid. Your macaroni and cheese will get cold."

My brother Brad and I pose with our dog, Lassie.

My horse's name was usually Trigger when it wasn't Silver or Champion (Dale's horse was Buttermilk and the dog was Bullet when I included them in my make-believe) and every one of my death-defying escapades ended in my saving the day and riding off into the red sky—"Hi-yo, Silver! Away!" This is how I would leap into my bed at night.

"Hi-yo, Silver! Away!"

"Are you going to sleep with your hat on, pardner?"

A six-year-old king of the cowboys!

"I'll take it off later."

"Tom, cowboys don't sleep with their hats on."

"All right, I'll take it off."

"Good night, dear."

"Good night, Mom." And I went to sleep with my feet beneath the blue and white Mickey Mouse sheets, still wearing my boots.

It had been almost a year and a half since my father had left for Korea. He wrote letters home telling Mom how bored he was. Korea was the only place he had ever been where the minute he got off the plane, he began to count the days when he'd return. Mom sent him pictures of the family and boxes of her chocolate chip cookies.

Then one day he came home.

It was Christmas time and we played our 45 rpm records of Gene Autry singing "Rudolph the Red-nosed Reindeer" and "Santa Claus Is Coming to Town" and made long lists of the toys we couldn't live without.

And in the midst of it all was a stranger, tall, sober-faced, back from Korea, somehow unrelated to the sounds and smells of a family Christmas in Illinois where there were no ravages of war. There had been 165,485 U.S. casualties in the Korean War; 54,246 dead.

But Korea was only a word to me, like the words Pearl Harbor and Axis and Hitler. When I played war with my tanks and guns I could always get out of my foxhole and eat lunch or ride my bicycle down the block. I didn't know about the armistice signed at Panmunjom in July 1953, which brought my father home again. But now he was here. And I realized there were other places in the world, terrible places, and my father had been there.

After Christmas my father received new orders. This time we would be moving to Minneapolis, where he would be an advisor to the Minnesota Army Reserve Forces.

It was an icy January morning when we left for Minnesota. Grandpa tucked two one-dollar bills into my pocket, "in case dere's anything open for you to buy a little something in the Wisconsin Dells," and he gave me a quick hug. I rode in the back of my father's Oldsmobile with two large thermos jugs, a box of house plants packed in crumpled newspapers, a pile of blankets, and my brother, Brad, who immediately tipped over one of the thermos jugs.

Wisconsin looked white and wind-bruised, and snow rippled across the highway as we drove through the silent cold. In the front seat Julie was whining about being hungry. We had been driving for several hours, and Brad had fallen asleep with his head pressed against the crumpled newspaper in the box of house plants. I watched the flat whiteness outside the window and wondered what Roy Rogers would do in a predicament like this.

"It must be 20° below," my father said dryly. "At least a 60°-below wind chill."

"When do we eat, Mommy? I'm hungry."

"Eat—nothing! I've got to go to the bathroom," came a sleepy voice.

"We'll stop at the next place we see," Father answered.

Unfortunately, especially for my brother, who had to go to the bathroom, we didn't stop until we reached a two-story white duplex 140 miles down the road. It was on Bryant Avenue in South Minneapolis, with snow piled high all around and huge icicles hanging from the windows.

"Well, here we are. Wake up, Brad. We're here."

"Do we eat now?"

There were still Christmas decorations in some of the windows in the apartment building across the street. Little green wreaths blinked on and off with red and blue lights. Someone had thrown a Christmas tree out and it rested on the curb by a trash can. Strings of silver tinsel shivered in the wind, and the snow, heaped high and white on the ground, was threaded with pieces of tinsel.

I buckled my sheepskin-lined cap under my chin.

"Come on, Brad, wake up."

"Good grief! He's got his head in the dieffenbachia!"

"Everybody out. You open the door, honey, and I'll bring the car around the back."

"Tom Junior, carry those blankets. Good grief, I can't get the door open. The snow is so high."

"Don't they shovel their walks here?"

"Brad, are you awake?"

Roy Rogers would ride right into the frozen wasteland, hat pulled down, shoulders squared, his trusty dog, Bullet, at his side, tromping through the tall drifts. . .

"You're dragging the blankets in the snow, Tom! Pick up that thermos, Brad. No, no, Julie, for heaven's sake, don't eat the snow."

We settled into our small duplex apartment and soon all our old familiar furniture rested comfortably in place throughout the rooms. I decided to dedicate myself to profitable accomplishments like memorizing what was on TV every hour of every day.

School was another story. I had various symptoms of anxiety regarding going to another new school. One of them was eating. I became Mr. Chubs practically overnight.

I would watch "Make Room for Daddy," eating banana splits and Hostess cream-filled chocolate cupcakes. I would watch the Texaco Star Theatre, giggling at Uncle Miltie, while eating dinner on a TV tray in front of the television set. "Flash Gordon," "Rama of the Jungle," "I Love Lucy," "Dragnet," "Fury"—I watched them all with my cap pistol in one hand and Mother's homemade fudge in the other.

My new teacher was a striking beauty with smooth cheeks and shiny hair. She wore blouses with round collars and full skirts with cinch belts at the waist. When she moved, she floated, and I was in love again. When I listened to Rosemary Clooney on the radio singing "Hey There, You with the Stars in Your Eyes," I imagined she was singing personally to me.

I had always wanted to do something heroic like Wyatt Earp or Marshal Dillon. Sitting on the flowered sofa, listening to my mom's humming in the kitchen, I would dream of doing great and noble deeds, but then I would always wonder for whom. Surely not the far away friends in Fort Bragg or Fort Benning—or the boys who performed daring tricks on the jungle gym back in Palos Heights, or for Miss Adams standing on a pillar of marble forever inscribed in my hall of famous beauties, or my father who had trod battlefields from Africa to Italy and had endured the barren, windswept countryside of Korea.

Who would ever notice me in this life?

I had no enemies and at the same time, I had no real friends. Mom said I thought too much. Dad said maybe I should go out for sports.

Sports. I felt about as comfortable with a baseball glove and bat as I would have felt on display in a wax museum. I didn't like baseball because I was never certain about the results. If I failed, how could I face people? Even then I was developing a certain dread of failure—though I wasn't even quite sure what failure meant.

If the Rifleman had the trials I did, where would he be today? I buried myself in constructing model airplanes and cars and dreamed of life like Jeff's on "Lassie" where Gramps was always there, loving, understanding, and through calm or storm there was a true friend like Porky Brockway, and across the field running toward me, *"Ee-yakee!"* would come the best friend a boy could have, his dog.

Our own real live Lassie came to us as a puppy and it was the biggest day of my life. I named her Lassie because she was a collie and because then I could be just like Jeff on TV. The whole family fell in love with her and soon she was like another member of the family. We even took her with us on our many trips to Chicago when we drove the nine-hour trip to my grandparents'. She'd sit in the back seat with me, Brad, the sweaters and thermos jugs, with her tongue dripping out of her mouth. I'd watch the flat earth, carpeted with wheat and corn, through the car window and dream of the adventures we'd share together.

Me and my dog Lassie.

Chapter
Five

I don't know when I started growing taller than everybody else. When I was eight I looked ten, when I was ten I looked twelve.

Tall, taller, and tallest.

My mom and her women friends, who put their hair up in pincurls with bobby pins and took sunbaths in the backyard, made giggly jokes about how I must be eating my spinach. Mom would joke back how she would buy me a pair of shoes and by the time we got home my feet would be ready for the next size already. Frankly, I didn't mind the attention. It made me feel more like a man. I decided I would be the type of man on "Father Knows Best," loving, wise, good, and kind.

Then we moved again and I was sent to another new school. This time the move took us to Bloomington, only a few miles away, south of Minneapolis proper. My parents bought a rambler with three bedrooms and a sloping front yard with two spindly silver oaks in nests of pebbles. I mused that if Ricky on "Ozzie and Harriet" thought *he* had troubles he should just live a few months in my life.

We needed three bedrooms because now my mom had given birth to another baby. It was a girl and they named her Wendy. She was a little pink bundle with squinty blue eyes and unbelievably tiny fingers and toes. Mom dressed her in white and pink lacy things and she occupied every room of the house. In the kitchen her bottles were lined up in rows on the counter, turned upside down, all sterilized and germ-free; in the living room were little piles of receiving blankets and Mom's sewing patterns for baby things; in the bathroom were her powders and oils and in my parents' bedroom the array of baby furniture. The only place she didn't actually occupy space was in the room Brad and I shared. Here my model airplanes hung from the ceiling like strange birds flying into one another, and our beds with the blue bedspreads with horse heads distinctly advertised: Occupied by Boys.

I was nine years old now. The gaps in my mouth were now occupied by white even teeth and I could spell words like Mississippi and Afghanistan and raisin.

My father was gone on maneuvers a lot and I would be instructed to "be the man of the house now." Although I wasn't exactly sure what that meant, I thought about it and took it seriously. I helped my mom feed her pink and lacy baby; I shook out the dusty rugs on the back stoop, watching the flecks dot the snowdrifts. I never left a ring in the tub after taking a bath and I turned out lights behind me.

In the Morning of My Life

One thing I think I've been aware of all my life is other people's feelings. I never wanted to hurt anybody if I could help it and I really enjoyed helping people. I was never the type who would shout, "Fatty, fatty, two-by-four" or anything cruel like that.

So I would always experience a familiar anxiety when changing schools. What if the kids were mean? I never liked it when they'd make fun of the teacher or get into fights. I was more of a peaceful type. And I always got along with grownups. My mom would be proud of me because I never forgot my manners when we had company, and I was always courteous when we went out anywhere. "That Tommy," her friends told her, "what a little gentleman. Why! He is the most polite young boy I've ever met. How did you do it?"

It's not easy being the most polite boy on the block. Especially when the neighborhood hero and his friends are bullies. Once, in Fort Riley, the neighborhood bully took my bike and hid it in a deep ravine. That's when I had my first fight—and it was a doozy. I don't think anybody won, but it was a long time before anyone wanted to fight with me again.

The best day of the week was Friday. I always knew it was Friday when the Mousketeers sang:

*"M-I-C—See you real soon—
K-E-Y—Why? Because we like you—
M-O-U-S-E!"*

Then they'd cheerfully wave good-bye for another week. Friday was Party Night at our house. That meant we could stay up as late as we wanted and watch TV. Mom would make fudge and we would have Pepsi-floats and watch old movies right up to the sermonette. With the playing of the Star-Spangled Banner, we'd stand and salute each other, giggling, until Mom shooed us off to bed.

Mom was big on birthday parties. Our birthdays were the most festive events of the year next to Christmas. In Bloomington she would decorate the basement to look like a French cafe. She'd hang streamers and balloons from the pipes in the ceiling and set little tables around and then the horde of children would sit wearing funny paper derby hats, posing for pictures. The girls came in their full skirts and black patent leather shoes, with their hair curled and barrettes at the temples, and the boys wore pressed trousers and striped sweaters, their hair clipped in crew cuts and shaved above the ears. We'd eat egg salad sandwiches and jello salad and drink bottles of Squirt and Dad's Old Fashioned root beer. Then mom would bring in the cake, all laid out on a baking sheet, a grinning chocolate snowman or a map of the U.S. with little flags. Many times Mom set little ceramic horses on top of the cake for my collection. When it was Brad's birthday she always made a cake with green frosting because he was born on St. Patrick's Day. Brad spent his entire childhood eating green birthday cakes.

On Christmas we were inundated with presents. Even Lassie got presents, gift-wrapped and with her name on little stringed tags. For Brad and me there were toy guns, helmets, canteens, tinker toys, fire trucks with ladders that reached your knees, doctor kits, wind-up cars. For the girls there were yellow-haired dolls that walked, puffy white fur muffs with matching hats, doll high-chairs, cribs, and little boxes with ballet shoes painted on top. We'd open our presents to the accompaniment of Tennessee Ernie Ford singing hymns in the background and on Christmas Day we'd eat turkey and dressing and pies with whipped cream on top.

In the fourth grade I was "discovered." I became the art talent of the class. I had been drawing pictures most of my life and nobody noticed anything unusual about it, but now Mrs. Stroth, my dark-haired, attractive teacher with the dimpled arms, seemed thoroughly impressed. "Why! Thomas, you draw very well! Let me see that."

Her pink dimpled arm reached across my desk. "Say! That's quite a picture you have there," and with a flap of the paper in her hand, she took it from me and tacked it on the wall.

Forever after through the year my pencil drawing of a blacksmith hung on the wall by the American Dental Association's poster of a bicuspid.

Mostly I drew horses. That was because horses were my favorite animals. I read the *Black Stallion* books as well as *Black Beauty* and *The Red Pony*, and I never missed a "Fury" show on TV. Life would have been wonderful if it could have been just a boy with his horse and his dog.

In April of 1958, right in the middle of fifth grade, we moved again—this time to Fort Riley, Kansas. My father, a major now, had new orders. We moved into the large stone officer's quarters, just four houses away from the house Custer lived in when he was at Fort Riley.

I gritted my teeth and went off to face another new school.

Everything at this new school seemed. to be Space. Space, Space, Space. There were photos of rocket ships all across the front of the room, and names for reading groups like Mars and Venus and Pluto. It seemed that we were forever in our little science satellite learning about galaxies, comets, and planets. All the boys and girls in the room had pictures of suns and moons on their notebooks and dreamed of traveling in spaceships one day.

I spent the first month in Fort Riley playing Monopoly, Go to the Dump, Crazy 8s, and Checkers with Brad. One day we talked Mom into playing Monopoly with us. She sat purse-lipped, studying the pieces on the board, and I tap-tapped my fingers and looked out the picture window at the little knot of boys playing together outside. I was being cautious before making friends, before entering into their Fort Riley world. Then one day I saw some small heads wearing army helmets pass by the picture window, followed by another and another. They had canteens strapped around their waists and carried toy rifles. In hot pursuit, not far behind, came two or three more boys wearing army fatigues with bayonet sheaths at their hips. That was it. I leaped out of the kitchen chair and ran to the door. "Come on, Brad!" I called, leaving Mom just as she was about to put a hotel on Marvin Gardens.

Soon I had friends. Michael Leddy, a curly-haired boy my age, became my best friend. We

Julie, me, Wendy, Brad, and my birthday cake.

played army night and day. I had friends and I also had Brad, my brother.

Brad always wanted to do what the "big kids" did, but one day he went too far. I had found out about an art contest on TV. You had to draw a picture of the monster Rodan when it flashed on the screen, just from memory of that flash. The winner would receive a free ticket to the movies. It was a real challenge and I sat down at the kitchen table with my pencils and sheet of typing paper and drew the monster. It turned out pretty well and I left it on the table while I hunted for a stamp and an envelope.

Brad found the picture and traced it, line for line. He filled in all the shading and made it dark where I had pressed heavily with the pencil, lighter in the light places, then he signed his name and asked Mom for an envelope and stamp. Later I received notice in the mail that I had won—but so did Brad. He confessed that he had traced my picture. I was so angry I hardly even enjoyed the free movie. Brad just laughed that square-jawed, crooked little laugh that everybody loved so much and that was all there was to that.

So much for my big claim to childhood fame!

I forgave Brad later and just to prove it, played "Red Rover" with him and his friends. I played on his side so he'd win. Being tall made me a great runner. But it was easy to see that Brad would be the real athlete in the family. He was built tough and strong, and when he played he put all his energy into it.

The reason I didn't play too many games was that I hated to lose. I just couldn't stand not having things under control. I wanted to know what to do, how to do it, and then I'd do it as well as I could. Games had such an element of chance involved. I just wasn't attracted to games.

Chapter Six

What I did like was roller skating. On skates I could zip along like a hot knife through butter. I practiced in the basement of our house in Junction City, rounding the corners by the furnace on two wheels, turning circles in the middle, racing backward on one foot and then the other, whipping around the support beams with a foot in the air, the smell of cement dust and damp brick in my nostrils. I'd play Mom's Jackie Gleason records on the big box phonograph with silhouettes of people dancing on the front and big black eighth notes on top. Then my friends would come over with their skates and the house would sound like an armored tank invasion.

When the Soviet Union sent a rocket orbiting around the earth and the United States sent two monkeys up in the nose cone of a Jupiter missile, we were skating around in circles in the basement.

And I entered the world of art. "Tom, that's just precious," my mom would tell me when she'd survey my latest paint-by-number portrait of some amber and gray-colored horse. I'd hang these works of art over my bed by the shelf with my model horses and model cars.

When Dad would go on maneuvers, Mom would pack us up in the car and we'd go to Chicago to visit my grandparents. I'd sit in the front seat with Mom and Wendy and Julie, and Brad would sit in the back with Lassie, the jackets, and the thermos jugs. At my grandparents' house we would play and make loud noises, and tell stories that would always receive a chuckle of approval.

"Dad, what's black and white and red all over?"

"Aw, Tommy, I know that one. A newspaper."

"Nope. A skunk with a sunburn. Ha! Ha!"

Then one bright morning in June I entered the Junction City business world—the world of responsibility and finance. I landed a job at the supermarket, bagging groceries. I decided to deposit my earnings in the First National Bank to build for my future, whatever that meant.

"You've got to build for your future, Tom," my dad had told me. "Put a little away for a rainy day." I didn't know why money would be any more valuable in the rain than in the sun but I stood in line at the officer's desk in the bank anyhow.

"I would like to open an account."

"All right. And what is the amount of the deposit, please?"

"$2.80. Cash."

While working as a bagger I put oranges and Kleenex and pork chops and TV dinners into the bags and dreamed of Martha Seitz, the prettiest girl in Junction City. She had long brown hair and the whitest smile I ever saw.

When school started I felt the familiar fog of dread again, as though my life were taking place somewhere other than everbody else's. The other boys and girls in the sixth grade were in one place giggling and telling stories and playing games, and I was in another, tall and sighing, fearful of making a fool of myself. I did well in school. I knew the answers to questions, I handed in my book reports on time, and always I worried that someone would whisper "Show-off!" in my ear.

But in music class we had dances. The teacher would bring her Les Paul and Mary Ford records and the boys would stand on one side of the room and the girls on the other. Then we'd dance. I'd never danced in my life except for step-hop step-hop to my grandparents' polka records. But standing by the opposite wall, looking directly at me with an expectant sweet smile, was Martha Seitz. Somehow my feet moved all by themselves, and she danced with me.

I floated through the next days. Martha Seitz, the *femme fatale* of the sixth grade, liked me! I began to walk a little straighter, talk a little more, and one morning I bravely entered the high jump contest in the Junior Olympics.

Out in the moist early morning, our breath white in the air, the contest gradually narrowed down to two of us. The other boy ran, jumped, and knocked the bar off its perch. Then I ran and leaped as high as I could and cleared the bar. I had won!

I was now a school champion. I don't know how it happened, when all I did was run and jump, but suddenly my life had meaning and purpose. The sixth grade in Junction City, Kansas, had to be the best place in the world to be.

One Sunday morning when my mom was out in the kitchen stirring up some Aunt Jemima pancakes, I watched Oral Roberts on TV and I suddenly felt very strange, as though he were speaking directly to me, personally. He was talking about God and about how we were created to know him. I didn't know much about God, except the Lord's Prayer, though I did go to Sunday school occasionally, and we had *The Bible in Pictures for Little Eyes* on the shelf, but somehow this was different. I felt confused, afraid. I went into my bedroom and rummaged through my collection of *National Geographics* and found my little blue Bible with my name in gold on the cover that I had gotten from my Gramma Netherton. I didn't know where to read but I turned to the Gospel of Matthew. I just sat there and read. The words were like darts. "Blessed is he who searches for righteousness for he shall be filled. . . ."

Then Mom called me to breakfast. "And Tom, don't forget you have to baby-sit for the Aarnts this afternoon."

"OK, Mom."

"What's wrong, dear? You look funny."

"Nothing's wrong, nothing. . . ."

Chapter Seven

By the time I was in the seventh grade, I was quite the dancer. I'd dance along with "Your Hit Parade" and records of Johnny Mathis and Mitch Miller. Now not only Martha Seitz liked me, but some of the other girls in school did, too.

By now my birthday parties had become dance parties and Mom would decorate the basement in streamers and little paper lanterns and we'd eat sloppy joes and dance to Frankie Avalon, Dion and the Belmonts, Marty Robbins, and Paul Anka. The girls wore pleated skirts and ankle socks and the boys wore corduroy pants and turtleneck sweaters and our favorite song was Mark Dinning's "Teen Angel."

Caryl Chessman was executed at San Quentin that year, the Salk vaccine was wiping out polio, Cuba signed a trade agreement with the Soviet

Union, and I was unanimously declared the winner of the seventh-grade twist contest.

The reason I won was that I was tall and could move around well and also because the girls in the class all voted for me. I was no longer worried about getting too good grades and people making fun of me. I gave up Martha for Dinah Rose, an Older Woman in the eighth grade who walked with a slow, quiet kind of walk and talked about things like modern architecture and taking the Northern Pacific to Seattle to listen to the rain.

But then in eighth grade right after Easter, when I got a new silvery sport jacket to wear to church, we received news that sat like ice cubes on my spine. We were going to move again.

Back to Minnesota.

The boxes of tea cups and Tupperware were stacked atop boxes of winter clothes marked *W* in magic marker, and summer things marked *B* for basement. The china cabinet was wrapped in a padded quilt, our beds were taken apart, and the chipped and scratched headboards were standing up straight against the side of the moving van. A box on the stoop held my collection of books, *The Black Stallion and Flame*, *Black Stallion's Courage*, and *The Island Stallions*, packed in with Mom's *The Silver Chalice*, *From Here to Eternity*, and *Look Younger, Live Longer*.

"For heaven's sakes, are you going to stand there staring all day like that? Come, Tom, get a move on."

Our Doris Day records stuck out of a box too small for their edges to be covered. Mom was pushing aside a box of food from the refrigerator to

Top left: **Me, in 1960.** Top right: **Major Netherton, my dad, in 1961.** Bottom: **Vacationing in the Wisconsin Dells.**

give to the lady next door and buttering slices of bread for peanut butter and jelly sandwiches.

"Will you mix up some Koolaid, Tom? For the thermos. Say, don't you feel well?"

Oh, sure, I felt just fine. Who wouldn't feel fine when his whole world was going down the tubes?

Now I'd have to start all over again. Another new school, new teachers, new kids, and there I'd be, standing awkwardly at the front of the room, handing my report card to my new homeroom teacher again. It seemed as if my whole life was spent handing old report cards to new teachers. And the sea of strange faces would stare at me, the boys in their V-necked pullovers and the girls wearing poppit beads and birthstone rings.

Here, Miss Whatever-your-name is, here's my report card. Notice the A's and please, dear God, don't let everybody laugh at me.

"Did you add the sugar?"

We moved back to Bloomington. Well. That was a comfort. At least I knew the names of the streets and I could make comments like, "What do you know, there's a 7-11 on that corner now," or something adult and lucid like, "Why! I remember when this neighborhood was just an old grassy field."

I went to Penn Junior High and threw myself into my studies. Not that I loved studying. I mean, I really wasn't concerned with 106 to the tenth power or the irrigation systems of the Negev in Israel but it was a way of grabbing hold. I produced results, I was in control. It was like showing myself that I really did exist in this world.

Sometimes I think the true geniuses of all time are the ones who handed in eighth grade papers with black smudges and eraser marks and never got anything more than a C in algebra because somehow when it comes time for them to invent something brilliant or perform some incredible high task, they throw their whole heart into it and it turns out meaningful and wonderful. Me, I sat at the head of the class without a shred of my heart connecting to anything.

Until later.

Talk now was about the U.S. cutting diplomatic ties with Cuba and the anti-Communist Cuban refugee invasion landing at the Bay of Pigs. Kennedy was our young and exciting new president and all the girls wore Jackie Kennedy clothes and hairdos.

My new heroes were Maverick, "Riding the trail to who-knows-where, luck is his companion, gambling is his game . . . ," Danny Thomas, and Mr. Ed, the talking horse. Sometimes to cheer myself up I'd go down to the basement and listen to old Spike Jones records or some of the newer Shelly Berman and Bob Newhart albums.

Better than anything would be a trip to Chicago to see my grandparents.

Chapter Eight

"Well, now! My little feller's not so little anymore!"

"I grew two inches, Dad."

"You sure did. More like four. More like a foot!"

"Aw—"

"One a dese days you'll be taller than me. Yessir. One a dese days. Say, you put on a little weight, too!"

"Oh—"

"Uh huh. Well! You like school, Tommy?"

"Yes, sir."

"You getting good grades?"

"I guess so."

I just really want to jump into your arms, Dad, and tell you I love you. I'm still your little feller. Taller, but I have things to say—words somewhere in my head, like sunlight ready to spill out. I want to say things—important things like about the day you bought me my first three-

*wheeler, and about how I like to see you stand-
ing here in the stubby grass watering it with the
hose on "spray."*

"Would you like a glass of apple juice?"

"Yes, sir."

"And how about Brad? Is he thirsty? Now where
are the little ones? Julie! Wendy! Where'd they go
off to now?"

At night, lying on the mattress on the floor of my
grandparents' living room with my brother asleep
next to me, I'd think about words that go unsaid.
But then I'd drift to sleep to the sound of the Reg-
ulator clock and the buzzing of the window fan
in the dining room. The moonlight streaming
through the living room window revealed my picture sitting on the mantel. My face was up there in
the shadows and the forest of other frames, a
toothless first-grader who would one day be a little
feller no more, but who would always want a hug
from his grandpa.

Chapter
Nine

Starting the ninth grade isn't so horrendous when you have someone you can say hi to when you get there. I actually knew someone! I even walked to school the first day with two other boys my age.

By now I was adjusting to being in one place for awhile. I went out for swimming and track that year and began to enjoy my studies a little bit more. I discovered the guys wanted to hang around with me and, wonder of wonders, the girls noticed me, too.

I went to roller skating parties, hay rides, pizza busts, wienie roasts, and record hops. We had dance parties in my basement and we ate hot dogs and Fritos and drank Pepsi-Cola and danced to Pat Boone and Neil Sedaka.

We watched "American Bandstand," chewed Beechnut spearmint gum, and by my own choice I didn't drink or smoke; if there were drugs around, I didn't know it.

I guess I could have chosen a rough crowd, but I didn't. My mom asked me if my friends smoked or drank and I told her simply, "No. We don't have to."

More than anything, I wanted my life to count for something. Deep inside I worried that I'd never amount to much.

Our family was religious, but only in the broadest sense of the term. I sat in hundreds of church services, never really aware of anything spiritual going on. We'd have the opening hymn, the number by the choir, the Scripture reading, the offering, announcements, sermon, a final hymn, and then out we'd go. What it meant to me was wearing my gray polyester sports jacket and sitting still for an hour.

But one day for no reason at all I reached into the bookcase in my room and pulled out my Bible. I sat on my bed reading it.

I read in the book of Proverbs: "My son, listen to me and do as I say. . . ."

It was like that odd experience I had when I had seen Oral Roberts on TV, back in sixth grade. I got up and looked into the mirror. "I wonder if I'm a Christian," I thought, staring at my reflection. These were hazy, unsure thoughts because I didn't know exactly what a Christian was, except that he wasn't a Jew or a Moslem.

I didn't have a desperate need for God or any insatiable hunger to know him. I just wondered about things. I wondered, "What if I'm not a Christian at all . . . ?" Who was a Christian, anyhow?

I sat there reading for a long time. "My son, give me your heart, and let your eyes observe my ways."

What ways? I felt somehow hollow and filled at

the same time. Something was happening to me.
Even my skin felt strange. My arms were prickly
and bumpy like the skin of an orange.

> The Lord's wisdom founded the earth; his
> understanding established all the universe
> and space. The deep foundations of the earth
> were broken open by his knowledge, and the
> skies poured down rain. Have two goals: wis-
> dom—that is, knowing and doing right—and
> common sense. Don't let them slip away, for
> they fill you with living energy, and are a
> feather in your cap. They keep you safe from
> defeat and disaster and from stumbling off
> the trail (Proverbs 3:19–23, *The Living Bible*).

I went to Youth Night at the church we were
attending, and while we were skating around in
circles in the roller rink, keeping time to Frank
Sinatra records, I heard the words over and over
again in my head, "My son, give me your
heart. . . ."

Chapter Ten

Two of the prettiest girls in school were twins named Peggy and Vicki. They were popular, sought after, and always seen leaning on a locker with some baseball hero or student council president. I didn't have the nerve to ask one of them out. It was Peggy I really liked. She had straight auburn hair that curled up at the ends and deep blue eyes that looked right into your head. When she looked at me I felt as if she could read my mind. Finally I worked up the courage to ask her out. It was time for the Fall Hop, perfect opportunity.

"Peggy—" I began artfully, "are you doing anything the night of the Fall Hop?"

"I beg your pardon?"

"Well, Peggy, I think you are the most super girl in the whole school."

"Really? Me?"

"Oh, yes, you. Peggy, I was wondering if you'd like to go to the Fall Hop with me."

Her reply was icy. "I'm Vicki."

I went to the Fall Hop with Jane Thompson, one of the girls from our hay-riding and wienie-roasting gang. She was a very sweet girl, one a guy could talk to about important things like Kennedy's inaugural address and Pogo cartoons.

I gave up the swimming team when I decided it wasn't worth all that gasping for air and gulping chlorinated water into my lungs. I ran track, though, a singular sport. I still wasn't interested in team sports. Every once in a while when I looked at one of Brad's baseball gloves I'd get a flashback of an experience back in Palos Heights, and it would all return again. So painful. Back in the third grade, wherever it was, I was out on the baseball field. I still hadn't learned how to play baseball and there I was, out on the field, and I kept missing the balls. At bat I couldn't hit a thing. And one of the boys yelled, "Get off our team, Netherton! You're nothing but a tin soldier."

A tin soldier. All my fears confirmed! Never again will I try anything new or anything I'm unsure of in front of people, I thought. They won't let you learn, won't give you a chance to learn. A tin soldier! He called me a tin soldier.

I moped over that one for months. But here I was, a high school sophomore and I had never played another game of baseball. Swimming, track, tennis, skiing, yes—because I'd be on my own, by myself, an individual, and I could practice alone so nobody saw if I didn't measure up.

Speech was another thing. The first time I had to give a speech in Speech One it seemed more like a death sentence than a class assignment. I wrote out every word, every breath and pause. I drew little arrows up and down on the words where my voice was to be raised or dropped.

I was amazed when my speeches drew admiration from teachers and the rest of the class. "Cool, Netherton, real cool."

"Thanks."

(Whenever someone paid me a compliment I always wondered if he didn't mean someone else, like my walking up to the wrong twin and asking for a date.)

Pretty soon Speech became my "thing." I was knowledgeable on world events like tax hikes, the nuclear test ban treaty, and the space program, so I gave these informative, dazzling speeches. Nobody realized that I had every gesture and word meticulously planned beforehand.

I secretly envied the person who could just get up and talk fluently without spending half the previous night rehearsing in front of the hall mirror. Of one thing I was certain: I'd never be a public person.

That year my high school was presenting *South Pacific* for their annual musical production. I went to see it with some friends and sat on the edge of my seat through the whole thing. I could hardly believe the performers were people I saw in the school halls and cafeteria every day. There they were, singing and dancing, no longer high school juniors, but Nellie Forbush and Emile DeBecque holding hands and singing "Some Enchanted Evening" with a full orchestra playing. I could hardly imagine where they found the courage to stand up there like that on the stage.

For months afterward, I looked at those brave juniors as musical superstars. Stars, like Mary Martin and Ezio Pinza. Or Julie Andrews and Robert Goulet.

Early in the autumn my grandparents came to visit us. The whole family ran out of the house to meet them, including Lassie. They were getting older, but were still strong and healthy. I could hardly wait to sit down with my grandpa and talk to him, and to hear his husky voice and gentle laugh. "Yup, Tommy, you're quite the feller."

We made plans for Christmas when we'd visit them in Chicago, and we talked on and on into the evenings. Julie, Wendy, and Brad clung to them, as I did. The house was filled with laughter and their special sounds. Nobody argued and there were none of the stern silences that had been developing between my mom and dad.

Then they left, as they had done many times before. But this time was different. We kissed them good-bye in the driveway. We said good-bye things like Drive Carefully and Be Sure to Write When You Get Home.

They never reached home.

A car hit them in LaCrosse, Wisconsin, and they ran into the steel grating of a bridge. We received the call from the hospital that night.

None of us spoke on the trip to LaCrosse. We sat like pins in a bowling alley waiting to be knocked down. All of Grandma's teeth were knocked out and her little round face was a mass of bruises and cuts. Her hip was broken, as well as both wrists and both knees. She was hurt worse than Grandpa. He had some internal injuries and six

My mother with my grandparents, on their fiftieth wedding anniversary.

broken ribs but the doctor said he should recover readily. He lifted his hand and smiled when we entered his room. "It's OK. Now. Now. It's OK. . . ."

Mom and Dad went to LaCrosse faithfully three times a week (and we kids went as often as we could), until it was time for them to leave the hospital.

One awful day in November I was in my World History class when the loud speaker buzzed. It was the choked voice of our principal: "Students, teachers, we interrupt you with this message: President Kennedy has just been shot." We froze in our seats. Kennedy shot? Impossible. Some of the girls began to moan. We just sat in our seats, not moving. Then the principal's voice returned and we were excused from school. Later we heard the news that our President was dead. Assassinated. Radio and television relived the assassination over and over again. The funeral proceedings filled every U.S. living room. The grief was so heavy and horrible, it seemed there was no end in sight. I had never felt such hopelessness and despair in my life.

Grandpa was back in the hospital with prostate problems and one afternoon we received an emergency telephone call from my grandma. "You'd better come," she told us. "Doesn't look good at all." Still under the shadow of Kennedy's death, we rushed back to Chicago.

The hospital smelled of things sterilized, of sickness. I felt uneasy when we entered the revolving doors, like something dreadful was waiting for us. My mom's sisters were already there, standing outside his door in a huddle, weeping.

"Dear Lord, is he all right?" my mother cried.

"Go in and see him. . . . Go. Now."

We went in one by one, and fanned out around his bed. He looked thin, shrunken. His dear body was stretched out in a narrow lump under the white coverlet and there were tubes running into his arms.

"Dad . . ."

He smiled weakly at each of us, his "little ones." I was the last one out of the room. I took his hand.

"Tommy. . .?"

"Yes, Dad. Dad—I love you." I was crying.

He winked up at me, focusing on my face. ". . . still my Tommy, my little feller. . . ."

Then we were leaving, walking down the long gray hall, when we heard a voice. It was a nurse calling to my parents.

My grandpa was dead.

Chapter Eleven

Dead.

Just like that, gone forever from this earth. All the people in the world, crowding in airports and bus stations, filling the streets and the sidewalks, and as long as I lived, none of them would ever be my grandpa.

Somehow we went on eating and sleeping and living, but there would be a hole in my life that would always go unfilled because there was only one man to whom I would ever be "little Tommy," only one man who would ever think of me as his "little feller" and he was gone forever.

A few days later we were at my grandparents' house for the funeral preparations. I was sitting in the big armchair watching the news when suddenly I saw Lee Harvey Oswald shot. I hollered to the rest of the family. "Oswald's been shot right before my eyes!" Life seemed to have turned into a nightmare.

My grandma never was the same after Grandpa died. The sparkle left her and she never seemed to regain her enthusiasm and zest for life.

By now I was pretty well established in school. I had friends who liked me, teachers who respected me, and I was in a number of activities. Every once in awhile I'd hear some girl giggle and whisper remarks like, "Oh, look, there he *is*, isn't he *cute?*" And when I'd turn to see who they were talking about, there'd be nobody there but me.

Amazing.

In the spring I took drivers' training, and on a windy day in April, I passed the drivers' test. It was one of my major triumphs. I drove our 1957 Ford alone for the first time with the pride and determination of A. J. Foyt winning the Indianapolis 500.

Now I was really a man of the world. I could drive to school, pick up my dates in a car, go places, do things; yes, I had the keys to the kingdom now.

I learned how to do Latin dancing, and when our Spanish Club had a party, I was practically the only guy who could do any of the dances, so I danced nonstop all night with every girl, including Mrs. Kiriluk, my favorite teacher. I didn't care one bit for the guacamole or the burritos; I was the best dancer there and enjoying every minute of it.

Then in my junior year, my courage built up and, more brave than I'd ever been, I auditioned for the class play, *Arsenic and Old Lace.* I got the part of Jonathan, a monster.

I probably got the part because I was so tall, almost 6'5" by now. I was so excited about this theatrical adventure that I put everything I had into the part. I remembered the juniors of last year and how star-struck I had been over them, and I thought, "Now here *I* am, standing on the very stage *they* stood on. Me, Tom Netherton, an actor in a real play—on the stage!" You'd think I was Laurence Olivier starring in *Hamlet* or Alec Guiness in *Bridge over the River Kwai.*

My family came to see me perform. It was a real event. *Me* in a play, and in a major part.

On opening night I heard the squeak of the rope sweeping the curtains apart and there I stood waiting in the wings for my entrance, my heart beating so fast I could hardly breathe. Suddenly I panicked. *What have I gotten myself into? I must be crazy. There is an entire auditorium of people out there and I'm standing here waiting to throw my life down the tubes when I make a complete fool of myself. I wish there would be a tornado or a flood or at least a power shortage so I wouldn't have to do this thing! What are my lines? Good grief, what do I say?*

"Jiminy Christmas, Tom, you look awful. Are you sick?" It was the leading lady, dressed in her wig and long dress.

"Oh, no. I'm fine. Fine. Break a leg now."

(Break a leg is what they say in the "big time." Performers in the "big time" never say "good luck" to each other, they say, "break a leg." My music teacher told me that. She had played piano once in a bar in Kansas City so she knew about things like what show folk say to each other.)

Dear Lord, I think I'm going to faint. Tall people do not faint. Our Father, which art in heaven, hallowed be thy name. . .

When it was over, my family drew around me,

hugging me, kissing me on the cheeks, and telling me how terrific I was. We went out afterward for triple treats and turtle sundaes at Bridgeman's and Mom said, "Oh, Tom, you're just a natural for the stage!"

"You're kidding."

"No, I really mean it."

Brad watched me with a serious face. "For sure, Tom. You're just a real natural."

I just laughed.

Chapter
Twelve

In my junior year of high school, I was chosen by the American Field Service to represent the United States as a foreign exchange student. I would be sent to Peru.

"Peru! Good grief, what will you do over there?"

"Learn the culture, practice the language, be an ambassador for my country. . . ."

"But, I mean, Peru! You hardly even hear of it. Where is it, anyhow?"

"South America."

"Well, take along those little drops to purify the water. Suppose they kidnap you?"

"*Kidnap* me? What would they do that for?"

"Well, you never know. I've heard of those highway bandits in Latin American countries."

"Mom, it will be OK. It's approved by the United States government. I was chosen out of hundreds of applicants nationwide. It's a great honor."

"Oh, Tom, I'm *so* proud of you."

I couldn't remember a time in my life when Mom wasn't right there encouraging me in everything I attempted. It didn't matter what it was. I was sure if I chose to do absolutely nothing with my life she'd marvel at how I did it better than anyone else. She was, without our really knowing it, the brightness of our lives. It was her laughter, her energy, her ability to make drab things colorful that fed each of us children. I overheard her one day talking to a friend on the telephone. "The sound of that back door slamming is music to my ears," she bubbled. The person on the other end must have asked why on earth. Mom answered happily, "One of my *children* has come in, of course!"

She never tired of sewing badges on Scout uniforms, making fudge, driving us places, cooking our favorite meals, listening to our noisy fun, picking up socks. We fed her, too; we were the brightness of her life.

In June of 1964 we drove to the airport where I would board my flight for Florida, change planes, and fly to Lima, Peru. Mom, Brad, Julie, little Wendy, and Dad stood with me in the airport waiting area before boarding. We wore good-bye kind of smiles and said things like Be Sure to Write, Now, and I'll Miss You, and Take Care of Yourself, Now. Mom wore a little round hat and white gloves and was crying; Brad was watching the planes outside on the airstrip, and my dad was wondering how he was going to pay the $800 this trip was costing him.

Seventeen hours later I was in Peru.

Chapter
Thirteen

The plane from Miami made stops in Panama and Colombia, where other exchange students got off. There weren't many of us going to Peru— about ten, I'd say. I sat with a high school senior from Boston who talked about the girls he'd met last summer at Martha's Vineyard and the XKE he was going to buy as soon as he got his driver's license.

"Those babies sure can go."

"Sure can." (I had never even met anyone who drove an XKE.)

I craned to see the mountains out the window. They looked like crumpled paper from where we were.

"Old stuff," Boston said. "If you've seen one mountain, you've seen them all." (The closest to mountains I had ever seen were the hills surrounding the Wisconsin Dells.)

We finally landed and I couldn't believe that I was

actually in Lima, Peru! Lima was a modern city near the ocean, with tall white buildings, cathedrals, modern shops, and even a Sears Roebuck. There was a bridge separating the older section of the city, across the Rímac River from modern Lima, and they said millions of eggs were used in making the cement so the mortar would be harder. It was the bridge used in the novel, *The Bridge of San Luis Rey.*

My friend from Boston was more interested in the girls than he was in famous landmarks. When we viewed the Torre Tagle Palace, which housed the Peruvian Foreign Ministry, he sighed, "Seen one, seen them all," and when we strolled the Plaza de Armas, gazing at the government palace, the archbishop's palace, and beautiful city hall, he was clucking under his breath at various passing females. "Did you see that? Man alive. Outa sight!"

We were taken to the home of an American businessman who was in Peru working with the Peruvian Embassy. He had a daughter named Elizabeth who had eyes like black satin and skin the color of sweet butterscotch. Boston immediately went crazy over her. "I'm in love, man. I'm in love. Oh, this is going to be a great summer, I can tell you that."

That first evening we were taken to a basketball game where some Americans were playing. I stood next to an American army officer who seemed oddly familiar. Then I recognized him. Fort Riley! Colonel Klie, that was his name, Colonel Klie. I recognized him right off because he had a son my age, Bob, with whom I used to play army. Bob had bright red hair the color of the inside of an orange. All the Klies did. Even their eyelashes were orange.

And down there on the basketball court I saw my friend! He had grown taller and his red hair now covered his arms and legs, a film of orange fur all over him.

"I mighta known I'd run into you here," he shouted when he recognized me.

"Here, in Peru? Lima, Peru?"

"Well, why not? Sure. Why not Peru? Good gravy, man, you got tall."

"Yes. Well, I'm here as an exchange student. You here with the army?"

"My dad is a military advisor to the Peruvian government. I mean, how tall *are* you?"

"Six five."

"Man! Six five! I mighta known! Good old Tommy Netherton who always hated to play the bad guy. You play basketball, man?"

"No."

"You serious, man? You don't play basketball?"

"No. I go more for track, things like that—"

"Good gravy, man, you got tall. I mighta known."

We ate dinner on a magnificent terrazzo terrace with candles and lace and bottles of *agua mineral.* Gorgeous red and white flowers bloomed along the railings and walls. I noticed in the warm breeze that across the table, Elizabeth was smiling at me.

Our stay in Lima lasted only a few days and Elizabeth took me on a tour of the Plaza San Martín and the school in San Isidro, which really burned my friend from Boston. I allowed myself to float in her steady gaze and soft voice that pronounced Spanish without a trace of an American accent.

Some of the exchange students were to stay with families in Lima; others were going to jungle cities on the Amazon. I was heading for Puno, high in the Andes. Traveling with me would be my friend from Boston who was going as far as Arequipa, halfway up the Andes.

The *colectivo*, which was an old 1956 Ford taxi, arrived early in the morning to take us the 600-mile journey up the Andes. Our bags were heaped in the back with a few Peruvians and their babies and handwoven satchels.

Rocking back and forth over the gravel and potholes, we started off. "How long do you figure this trip will take?" Boston asked the driver.

"He doesn't speak English."

"Oh, just ducky. *¿Habla usted inglés?*"

"*No inglés.*"

"Just ducky."

We drove for hours; the Peruvians in the back chattered among themselves. I looked back once and saw a mother nursing her baby and quickly turned around in embarrassment.

Boston groaned in discomfort. We were sandwiched together in the front seat with the driver, a short little man who had the seat pulled forward so he could reach the pedals on the floor. My long legs were crunched sideways against the dash and Boston was curled up in the middle with his knees bent up practically to his chest.

Finally we stopped at a dusty clearing where a small adobe hut stood baking in the sun. Little children in dirty, ragged clothing ran around outside barefoot. They stood still in amazement when they saw us.

The driver pointed to his mouth and made eating motions with his hands.

"We're going to eat," Boston said brilliantly.

We stumbled out of the car, wincing with every step. Boston was sweating now and his face showed obvious distress. "My legs are broken. For crying out loud, my legs are absolutely broken."

Inside the windowless hut it was dark and hot. A blanket covered a door at the end of the room and there were a few goats standing around in the hay on the floor. A table and chairs sat in the center of the room. A man covered with sawdust and dirt hurried into the room.

"*Buenos! Buenos!*"

"*Buenos días,*" I said politely. Only the driver, Boston, and I were inside. The others stayed outside, leaning against the shady side of the house in the dirt. The driver spoke to the man in Spanish. The man nodded profusely, displaying bright white and gold teeth and vanished behind the blanket into the other room.

The driver motioned for us to sit down. My first inclination was to sweep the hay and other pieces of rubble from the chair, but I didn't want to insult anyone so I sat down with a crunch and Boston did the same.

"I'm dying of a headache," he said.

The heat closed in around us and even though it was dark in the room, I could see Boston's white pullover shirt was gray with sweat.

"What I wouldn't do for a Big Mac right about now," Boston said.

"Well, you can forget that."

"I just hope I get out of this alive. My head is killing me."

Our host suddenly emerged from the darkness; this time a gray, spotty towel was hanging from his forearm. He swirled a gray tablecloth that had probably once been white into the air and covered the table without even stopping to brush it off first. He still hadn't washed his hands and they were grimy with oil, dirt, and sawdust. He even had sawdust in the creases of his neck. He set a bottle of *agua mineral* on the table, then put down three greasy glasses.

"Oh, ducky," Boston said, rolling his eyes.

"*Por favor, señor,*" I said in my kindest voice, "*tiene usted refresco?*"

"*Refresco!* Ah! *Si! Si!* Coca Cola! *Dos?*"

"*Si. Si. Dos. Muchas gracias.*"

When the man brought us two Coca Colas in tiny bottles, Boston seemed somewhat relieved. "Ask and you receive, my friend," I said wittily.

When my eyes accustomed themselves to the darkness, I saw that there was a gray powdery dust covering everything. Shanks of straw poked through the walls. I remembered our instructions not to eat any fresh vegetables or fruit.

In a few minutes the man returned, carrying plates of fried bananas and rice. Then he placed a handful of flat bread rolls in the center of the table. He was covered with the same gray powdery dust that was on everything in the room. His beard, collar, shoes—everything about him—was dusty. Boston eyed his black, oily hands and then the bread rolls and shrugged.

"*Ah, mis amigos! Mis amigos!*" The dusty man chuckled, fluttering around the table in open delight.

We ate our food without saying another word and then I counted out the pesos to pay for our meal. When we stepped outside into the white, hot sun, I saw the others still sitting in the dirt eating out of bowls with their fingers.

The worst of the trip was yet to come. Eighteen hours up the mountains on narrow dirt roads over crags and holes; roads so poorly constructed you could hardly even call them safe footpaths. We met school buses loaded down with people, chickens, and cargo, rocking sideways along the ruts and ridges, their passengers hanging out the windows with nothing between them and a 2,000-foot drop into the canyons below.

"I'm going to die, I know it," Boston gasped. He clung to the dash with his hands until his knuckles were white. His legs stiffened, driving his feet hard into the floor. He looked as if he were having some kind of seizure.

"For crying out loud! Pull yourself together," I told him.

"Ask the driver how many people die on this road."

"I will not."

"Go ahead, ask. Just ask."

"Listen, I'm getting a little tired of your complaining. You haven't enjoyed one minute of this trip. If you die, we all die; now why don't you just pull yourself together and act right."

"Lordy! Here comes another one of those buses. The driver looks drunk! Just look at him! Oh, swell. This is it, I can tell. Man, this is doomsville."

Our driver put the car into reverse and we jerked backward. He aimed for a narrow ledge of gravel from which we looked straight down the mountain ledge. The school bus shifted gears and rocked past, honking, the chickens in crates on the roof squawking in the thin mountain air.

"Did you see how packed that bus was? They were standing in the aisles! Oh, this is suicide."

"Cut it out, will you? You're insulting our Peruvian friends."

"Here we are on death's doorstep and he says don't insult the Peruvians. Lordy!"

The eighteen long, tedious, and dangerous hours up the mountains seemed more like forever. Boston's skin was stone white when we reached Arequipa, our destination. His eyes were dim, like faded lampshades, and he looked as if he had shrunk. He asked, "What's that?" to no one in particular when he saw Misti, the giant, snow-covered volcano above the city. "Isn't it fantastic?" I said happily. "The only other one in the world like it is Mount Fujiyama!"

He gave me a sour look. "For crying out loud, Netherton," he said.

Then we gathered our bags, fumbling on weak knees and even weaker stomachs, and said our good-byes. He looked limp and sagging when he shook my hand.

"Here's where we part company," he said in a shaky voice. "Swell knowing you," and then we said things like Be Good, Ha Ha, and Take Care.

My journey wasn't over. I had a train to catch

and another 5,000 feet to go up the Andes.

Women were selling soup and chili from pots which rested on fires made in tin cans at the side of the railroad tracks. I bought a bowl of soup, smiling at a woman wearing a shawl and derby hat, and handed her some coins. She looked up at me as though she were seeing a mirage. For the most part, the Peruvians were small people, short and dark, and here I was, towering over them—all six foot five of me, and blond and hazel-eyed at that.

I found a seat on the train and watched the lights of Arequipa twinkling in the distance. At 8,000 feet the lights shone brighter than any I'd ever seen. Oh, Peru is a magnificent country, I told myself, as I leaned back in the seat. I was suddenly weary.

We made several stops, and it seemed that with every grunt of the train, I grew more weak. I looked around at the other people traveling with me and they were slumped in their seats, eyes closed, some of them snoring, others sitting feebly, unmoving, like balloons with the air let out.

At one of the stops a pleasant-looking middle-aged woman with cameras on her shoulder and *Suisse* stickers on her suitcase got on the train. She was such a contrast to the rest of us that I couldn't help noticing her. She sat upright in her seat, crinkling pages of a newspaper, alert and energetic. My left eye closed, my right eye stayed open. "Where on earth does she get the strength—?" She was at least forty years older than I, maybe more, and she was as bright and chipper as a young child. "Must be those *Suisse* stickers," I told myself. "She's from Switzerland. That's it."

Before I got to Peru the most rugged terrain I had ever seen were the foot-worn trails at Taylors Falls on the Minnesota-Wisconsin border where I went on our tenth-grade class picnic.

I got up out of my seat and staggered to the back of the swaying car and peered into the next car behind. It was filled with sleeping Indian men in straw hats and white muslin shirts. The women, also asleep, were barefoot and wearing black shawls, derby hats, and colorful big skirts. There were children, goats, pigs, all pressed into the car like potatoes in a bag.

We came to a stop and the little *Suisse* woman hopped off the train with her cameras. I watched her taking pictures of the Indians and the llama herd standing on the platform. I realized I wasn't breathing.

The train began scraping forward again and the woman bounded back onto the train. She smiled at me as she passed and I smiled faintly in return.

At the next stop, I saw tiny dancing lights on a huge body of water and I knew we were at Lake Titicaca. This was Puno, where I was to get off. I was now high in the Andes, 13,000 feet, to be exact.

A small, black-haired, mustached man entered the car with an anxious look on his face. He moved up the aisle and then looked at me.

"Tom?" he asked.

"*Si, señor*," I whispered.

He introduced himself as Sr. Alejandro Lira

Landa. (That last name was his mother's maiden name; they just called him Señor Lira.) He was to be my "father" for my stay in Peru.

"Are you at all affected by the high altitude?" he asked me in English. "Oh, no, sir," I answered in the brightest voice I could manage. "High altitude doesn't bother me."

We arrived at the Lira home somehow and I was taken to my room, up some stairs, right beneath the kitchen. Then I got into the small bed with the softest feather mattress in the world and, sighing and congratulating myself that high altitude didn't affect me in the least, I fell asleep instantly.

I didn't wake up for three days.

The house was on three levels. Each room was on a different floor. Mine was on the second floor. The kitchen was on the top floor, and while eating meals we could look down into the courtyard below and see small adobe shacks with chickens and pigs wandering around, barefoot dirty children with uncombed hair, and mothers carrying water in gray pails. The Lira family lived in splendor by comparison to most of their neighbors.

They treated me like foreign royalty, fussing over me and serving me and following me around. There was an Indian servant lady with long black braids who cooked the meals. She would stand grinning and wiping her hands on her dirty apron which she never washed nor removed the entire time I was there, smiling and smiling a wide, toothless smile at me. She had a little black derby perched atop her head and she wore it day and night.

Left: **Our maid in Peru (you get used to the derby after a while).** *Right:* **Dinner time on the totora weed island.** *Top:* **The view from our kitchen window in Peru.**

Top: **My Peruvian father, Sr. Alejandro Lira, and his little son.** Bottom: A Panamanian farmer on his way to market.

For the first few days, the Lira children stared at me without a word. The meals were a little awkward. The only one who didn't stare was Sr. Lira, who was doing his best to make me feel at home.

His wife spoke no English and I don't think she liked me very much. She had hoped they'd get a girl, but for some reason there weren't enough girl students and so they got me instead. By her anxious looks I reasoned that she was worried about her seventeen-year-old-daughter with dark somber eyes and long black hair.

We went to the town square, walking down crooked little streets with adobe buildings on either side that looked like they would collapse any minute. The people moved around on the little balconies and carried on their lives without a thought that their houses could crumble to dust at any moment.

The news of my arrival spread fast and I was the guest of honor at the Cultural Center, and at many homes. There was even a parade in my honor. The mayor, who was a Communist, didn't come to any of the celebrations, but the other officials did.

The wife of the visiting American ambassador to Peru told me I should go into the foreign service.

"But what makes you say that?"

"My dear, you are so—so *articulate*. And you are only sixteen years old. You *converse* so well. Yes, the foreign service would suit you very well."

Naturally I thought she was simply being kind.

At one of the parties I met the most stunning girl I had ever seen in my life. She looked like Sophia Loren in the movie, *Breath of Scandal*. She was at most of the parties that they held for me and she was the only one I wanted to dance with.

My schedule was full with teaching English at the Cultural Center, sitting in the classes in the high school, the parties and dances, and traveling to see the majesty and mysteries of the land.

One of those mysteries was Lake Titicaca, the highest navigable body of water in the world. There was an Indian civilization, the Uros, built right on the water of totora weeds. It amazed me. The Indians built little islands by laying these weeds in the water until they had a surface and then they built huts of totora on top and lived there. They raised babies, slept, ate, and lived out their lives that way. When the water started seeping up and over them they built another island. Hardly like life back in Bloomington where green shaved lawns were dotted with little plaster statues of coachmen and roosters among beds of daisies and petunias.

One of the most breathtaking experiences was the trip to the ancient city of Machu Picchu which perched on a 2,000-foot cliff above the Urubamba River. We got there by a single-car train that traveled over the five switchbacks reaching out over the Cuzco valley. The walls of the valley are almost vertical, and after we reached the end of the line we had to travel the rest of the way in a clacking, careening bus along a dizzy road with dozens of hairpin curves to the summit. I couldn't understand how the Incas ever got up there to build their city.

I began to feel that people, that is, the human race in general, were capable of brilliant accomplishments, more brilliant than we knew about. I wondered if I would find my own potential and fulfill it. I wondered how many people ever did. Look at the Incas.

The city of Cuzco was in a cuplike valley at an altitude of over 11,000 feet. By now I was becoming accustomed to the altitude and I took slow steps, didn't rush myself, and remembered to breathe deeply.

At one time the city of Cuzco was more magnificent than any city of Europe. Although modernized, it had changed very little from the colonial days and most of the people there were descendants of the Inca people. The Indians wore the same clothing they had worn for centuries.

I was served a plate of something that looked like spaghetti. Smiling, remembering my manners at all times, I began to eat.

"Do you like it?"

"Ah, *si! Me gusta.*"

"It's llama intestine."

The Uros Indians in Puno chewed the coca leaf to derive the cocaine from it. They had calluses on their feet an inch thick, rotten teeth, sickly bodies, and they lived on a diet of fish. It was a cruel survival for them. Most of them fished for a living; some of them worked in the tin mines in Bolivia, but whatever they did, they didn't make much money. They chewed the coca leaf to ease the pain of life a little.

I thought there must be a better way to find comfort. I felt very small in a world of enormous complexities. I couldn't look at these Indians with indifference. I felt somehow bound to them as if we were all in this human condition together and we were all in some mysterious unity, very important. But to whom?

Back in town, little children followed me in streams wherever I went. I hardly took a step without some small child underfoot. To them I was the Pied Piper of Hamelin, the oddity of the universe, the yellow-haired giant from the other side of the world. I'd grin at them, speak a little Spanish, and these gestures were like fanning the coals. Four more children would be added to my entourage and my knees would be rubbed with their little butterscotch-colored cheeks.

One of the teachers in the school I attended was a Communist and he often spoke against the U.S. He spoke only in Spanish and didn't think I understood, but I knew by the looks on the faces of the students and the steely glare he had for me that he was talking about my country. There were disputes about boundary waters and U.S. fishing boats coming into their offshore waters and again I felt very small, helpless.

The students asked me hundreds of questions all at once. Does everyone in America own a television set? Is it true you all have cars? Do all your children go to school? Why do your movie stars commit suicide? Was President Kennedy your greatest president? Do you have factories in every city? Does every house have a toilet?

One day the Lira family took me to the movies to see *West Side Story* playing in the little adobe movie house in the center of town. I was shocked at the response of the audience. The theater was full; in fact, some people were standing and sitting in the aisles. As soon as the movie began the audience began to titter with laughter. By the middle of the movie they were hysterical. When the movie was over I thought they'd have to be carried out in stretchers. They laughed so hard they were falling out of their seats. I couldn't figure out how such a poignant story could be so hilarious to them. They thought it was a scream to see tough guys dancing around the screen and singing songs. Singing to someone about hating him and wanting to kill him was just the funniest thing on earth. Even Sr. Lira was laughing. The children held their stomachs, with tears streaming down their faces. The rumble scene in the movie, where the Sharks meet the Jets, dancing and snapping their fingers, had them howling with laughter. I don't think Abbott and Costello could have been any funnier—or Chaplin, for that matter. Gang members just don't go leaping and pirouetting down the street.

Walking through the town, we passed little herds of llamas and I was careful not to get too near them. Their spit was like fire on the skin. They'd kick a person who got too near. Sitting at the table back in the Lira kitchen, I asked the name of the food we were eating.

"Llama tongue," was the answer. They get everything possible out of that poor animal, I thought.

Sr. Lira drove me to the train when it was time for me to leave Peru. They all kissed me and I promised I would never forget them. I had grown to love my "second family."

I stayed at the home of the same American businessman in Lima. Elizabeth was there, as beautiful as she had been at the beginning of the summer. The other students began arriving from their various cities and it was my friend from Boston who boasted the loudest. "Man, the parties! I had some ball!" Then he bragged about all the girls who were crazy about him and I felt the same way I did when I saw some Peace Corps people drunk at a party in Puno. Ashamed.

My family was waiting for me at the airport in Minneapolis. They stood there tall and clean and I rushed to greet them, carrying my llama rugs under my arm and Peruvian jewelry in my flight bag alongside the rolls and rolls of exposed film.

It will be many years before the smell of fried banana, the breathless feeling of the mountains, and the sight of the derby-hatted impoverished Indians will leave me.

Chapter Fourteen

That fall I returned to Bloomington High and was elected senior class president. I gave speeches and slide presentations on Peru throughout the whole year, and much to the delight of my Spanish teacher, was able to carry on entire conversations using correct verb tenses.

I decided to be an architect and began my second year of mechanical drawing. Actually, I would have preferred to be an artist but advice from my father changed all that. Being an architect probably would be the responsible thing to be, after all. So I replaced my oil paints and charcoal with compasses and slide rules.

But still hanging on the wall of my freshman home room was my oil painting of an old mill beside a carefully lettered poem by some British poet. I had spent two weeks on it and was going to throw it away, but my teacher rescued it, so there it was, still hanging from uneven squares of masking tape beneath the map of the United Kingdom.

Social life for me had never been better. I went to parties, dances, picnics, barbecues, movies, was involved in all the senior class planning, besides being a musical "star." My grades went down to B's and C's, and a couple of my teachers approached me with the fact that I was absent from their classes more than I was present. I was always polite, but I wasn't sure how to say discreetly that belonging and being happy were more important to me than sitting in their classes.

Maybe if I had really known God at this point of my life, things would have been different, but the fact is, many of us had stopped going to church. It was just too dull. There were the social things to do there, of course, but it lacked the strength, the attraction that was necessary to bring and keep us there. Simply and honestly, it lacked *God*.

We didn't hear anything about God or Jesus in church. We heard about being good and doing good, but preaching like that didn't have any life or vitality to it. We needed more. We were young, filled with energy and enthusiasm, and we needed guidance and purpose. At least I did.

I found it with my friends.

The crowd I was with didn't booze or chase around destroying things and I was proud to be one of them. I felt I was gaining a kind of identity and it felt good. What that identity was, I wasn't quite sure, but at least I wasn't lonely.

Christmas came that year with the little silver and blue wreaths on the doors, the lights in the windows twinkling on and off, and the garland of cards decorating the top of the bookshelf. It was our first Christmas without Grandpa. There were no smells of my grandpa's cigar that year and no Danish coffee cakes, either.

I began making plans to enter the University of Minnesota the following fall. My life was centered in the activities at school and my family was the backdrop of the set. Mom was designing and sewing her own clothes, Brad was learning guitar and was now a football and basketball star, and Julie was a Beatle fan and Wendy had one of the largest Barbie Doll collections in the Western Hemisphere. My dad, who was now retired from the army, was away from home much of the time, working hard to provide for his family.

President Johnson gave his State of the Union address in January and I watched it on TV, standing at the kitchen sink eating a Spam sandwich. Ever since I had begun taking Speech I developed an interest in politics. Our speeches had to be on current events and issues, so I made myself aware of what was happening in the world. There was the Vietnam problem looming up in the American consciousness, the race riots, the disputes over the Panama Canal, the laser beam, and the emerging abilities of the computer. We would lope along singing "King of the Road" and dancing to "Hard Day's Night," but it seemed to me that we ought to know what was going on in the world. After all, it was our world.

When I recited from memory Martin Luther King Jr.'s "I have a dream" speech for a girl friend, she said, "Well, lah-de-dah, Mr. Smarts." I asked her if she had ever taken a stand for human equality and she replied with a cheerful smile that she took a

My high school graduation picture, 1965.

stand for anything as long as it wasn't fattening or illegal.

I felt we should all make our voices be heard for a better and happier world. But I didn't know how to go about doing it. One of my friends, Gary Gamble, was also concerned with human affairs, progress, and making his own life count for something. He was even thinking about being a missionary. This baffled me. How in the world could a person bring the knowledge of God to anybody? They'd really have to know God first. It was a novel thought.

I played Curly, the lead role in *Oklahoma*, in the spring of my senior year and actually enjoyed it. I didn't need my friends to dare me to audition this time.

I was amazed at the response to my performance. People said things like, "You were great, Tom!" and "What a beautiful voice!" I was hardly aware that I could sing at all. But people actually enjoyed listening to me!

I enjoyed these performances. I began to feel good about being backstage, wearing the makeup, listening for my cues, standing and moving on the stage. It felt good. But I had no intention of ever trying it again.

My dad helped me prepare the commencement address that I was to give at my graduation. I delivered it smoothly and without error. I knew he was proud of me. Later Mom served lemonade, potato salad, baked ham, and banana bread at the graduation party on our lawn. Her friends, looking chic in their spring suits and square-toed, high-heeled shoes, asked, "Well, Tom, what do you plan to do now?"

Smiling, always remembering to be polite, I answered, "I'll be starting at the university in the fall," the way thousands of other high school graduates were doing on their lawns all over the country.

Chapter
Fifteen

The beautiful University of Minnesota campus stretched out before me as I stood on the steps of Northrop Auditorium with my Sociology book under my arm. There was an argument among three students on my left about the merits of Adlai Stevenson, who had died during the summer. Nearby, some other students were hotly debating U.S. involvement in Vietnam. A young man with a guitar was sitting on the steps, wearing a stocking cap and plucking out Bob Dylan's "Blowin' in the Wind." Two girls were singing along in harmony.

The leaves on the great elm trees lining the walks were turning brown and orange and I shuffled slowly down the steps and across the pavement to the auditorium at the Museum of Natural History, for Sociology 1001. I had begun the semester with enthusiasm, but in just a matter of weeks I had almost completely lost interest in my classes, the people, and student life in general. Maybe it was the newness of it and the fact that I was anonymous. I had felt secure in high school—there I had really belonged, but here I was alone and without motivation.

Sociology 1001 reminded me of church. The teacher could have been our preacher. I was bored. I really didn't care at all that there were 249,187 immigrants flowing into the U.S. in 1950. I didn't care how tall the Golden Gate Bridge was and I didn't care why the Macedonian Empire fell to pieces when Alexander died. If he had died of measles as a child there probably wouldn't have been a Macedonian Empire anyhow.

I was *so* bored.

My dad was now working at Gabbert's Furniture Store, and with his help, I got a part-time job as their "97" boy. The "97" boy was the worker who did odd jobs. I carried out parcels, wrapped boxes, moved furniture, swept floors, and delivered goods to various departments. Whenever a department needed something from some other part of the store they'd get on the intercom and call, "97." That meant me.

One night one of the girls invited me to a party and there I met a sparkling, attractive dark-haired girl named Susie. We got to talking and she told me she was a singer. I was impressed. "For a living?"

"Yes. I sing at the Edgewater Inn."

"What's that?"

"It's a supper club in Northeast Minneapolis, by the river. That's why they call it the Edgewater."

She sang in a group called the Edgewater Eight.

They performed numbers from musical comedies; good, clean family show, she said.

"I've been in a couple musicals myself."

"No kidding. Why don't you come down and audition for our show?"

The idea was ridiculous.

"Oh, I don't think I could do that."

"Why not? If you've had experience and all—what could you lose?"

The next day at Gabbert's, carrying lamps to the showroom, I decided actually to take Susie's advice. I called and made an appointment to audition for the producer of the show.

When Al Sheehan and Gary Schultz, the producer and director, told me they liked my voice, I was amazed. Then they told me they wanted me for the show. I couldn't believe it. Yesterday a "97" boy, today a singer in a night club. I began rehearsals almost immediately.

I had my classes at the university in the morning, rehearsals in the afternoon, and the shows at night. The Edgewater had a good reputation for performers and it was a respected job for people in show business. I made $85.00 a week, the most I had ever earned.

It didn't take long before I was feeling right at home in my work. I loved the music, the costumes, the choreography, and the other kids in the show were friendly and fun to be with.

Oddly enough they thought I was religious. Maybe that's because I didn't drink or smoke. Somehow, instinctively I knew it took more than not smoking or drinking to be religious.

One night I came offstage and was heading for

the dressing room when I saw some people waiting at the door. I didn't recognize any of them, so I went on into my dressing room and changed clothes to go home. When I came out they were still there. I smiled as I passed them and then one of the women said, "Ohhhh, Tom!" I turned, thinking maybe I knew her. She waved a piece of paper in the air and said, blushing, "We waited to get your autograph—would you mind?"

My mouth fell open. My autograph! They wanted me to write my name on a piece of paper to take home with them! Soon three or four more pieces of paper were raised to me and I was actually signing my name to them. Then they all left and I got into my new Oldsmobile convertible and drove home.

After only a few months I began to think about dropping out of school and taking singing seriously.

"Dropping school?" my father exploded. "You need your education to fall back on. Besides, what kind of life would you have as a singer?"

I went to rehearsal that next afternoon, those words tossing in my head, and I wondered if I really should be happy after all. Maybe I was fooling myself. This singing thing could be just a passing interest.

But with each show I knew my performing was improving. My vocal technique, stage movements, interpretation, styling—all seemed to be falling into place. I was gaining confidence in myself as a performer.

One of the best things that happened to me while working with the Edgewater Eight was a girl

named Xenia. She was older than I, an ancient twenty-one to my eighteen, but she was so beautiful, so sophisticated, and moved with such steady, sure movements, I was swept off my feet. Those first months singing with the group had me in a euphoric state between feeling happily stagestruck and nervously in love.

Susie told me, "Xenia really likes you. Why don't you ask her out?" We began dating and I felt I had found the woman of my dreams. This was it. Xenia forever. We talked about getting married, but I knew I couldn't consider marriage until I was sure what I was going to do with my life. She turned her beautiful face up toward me and smiled her soft, warm smile. "That's all right, Tom; I'll wait."

It was at the Edgewater that I first began singing to the ladies in the audience, a technique I would employ for years to come. I moved among the tables and sang to certain ones scattered throughout the front of the room. One night I was singing "If Ever I Would Leave You" to a lady who was absently cutting her meat, completely unaware that the spotlight was on her and that I was standing at her elbow directing a love song to her. I continued to sing and she continued to slice her meat. Then she suddenly looked up and turned her head to me in shock. I supposed she was so accustomed to the television set on during meals that I was just another sound coming from a box. She looked at me as though she were seeing an apparition. But then, nonplussed, she turned back to her meat and continued to eat. The audience was laughing by this time and I sang right along to the sound of her knife and fork clinking against her plate.

We had many hilarious experiences with quick changes and rushing out on stage, trying to find our places on the wooden cubes that were our set. Once my quick change wasn't quick enough and as the lights came up on stage, I was rushing up the step still buttoning my shirt. I stumbled and tripped, falling flat on my face with a resounding thud across the stage. Another time we were singing "England Swings Like a Pendulum Do" and dancing a frug. I knelt on one knee and heard a *r-i-i-i-ip.* My pants had torn mercilessly from the front to back.

Sometimes I would sing from a ladder, other times from a cube or from down front, or in front of a pillar. We did some energetic dance numbers and some of our staging got a little tricky, especially when we were all on the small stage at once. The performances were always good and we were well known in town for doing quality shows.

After nine months of performing at the Edgewater, a new show every three weeks, two shows a night, I made a big decision—one that would alter the course of my life.

"I'm going to enlist in the service," I announced to my family.

"You're what?"

"Oh, Tom!"

"Yes. I've decided to join the navy."

"The *what?*"

"Wait a minute, you two—"

"You're going to join the *what?*"

"Big Tom—Little Tom, please—"

"The *what?*"

102

My father was turning red. His eyes were glaring. "I heard what he said! He said the navy!"

"Well. Uh . . . I thought—"

"Did you hear what he said? He said he's going to join the navy!"

"Tom, you're not serious. With Vietnam and all. . ."

"OK, I won't enlist in the navy. I'll enlist in the army."

"Tom, why enlist at all now? There's a war going on."

"I feel I must, Mom."

My father turned his face to the wall, then looked back at me. "How could you think of enlisting in the navy after all I've—" He couldn't continue.

I realized I had really hurt him. "I just thought it sounded like a good idea. I'm sorry." I wanted to reach out to him, to tell him I would never want to disgrace him, that I was proud of him and his army career, that I wanted him to be proud of me.

But I didn't say any more and he didn't either.

Later I asked my mother, "Why is it so hard for Dad to accept my decision?"

She made a nervous gesture, then answered in a small voice, "Maybe because he's always wanted the best for you, and you know how he feels about the army."

She cried for days, not understanding my decision to go into the service. Every time I looked at her there were little puddles at the corners of her eyes.

I explained to her I wanted to go into the service to get it over with. I didn't know what I was going to do with my life and I might as well get the service out of the way. "Besides, Mom," I said, "I want to mature. I want to grow up. I want to know who I am."

You see, at the Edgewater I was feeling a familiar emptiness again. I was moving and doing and making motions and using space and creating sounds—but I wasn't finding myself. I didn't have a quiet place within me. I had looked at those audiences night after night and wondered, "What on earth am I giving them?"

People came to the shows to be entertained, to be amused, but when they left, what had I really given them? I hadn't done anything that would necessarily mean much in their lives in the long run. People want to be loved. I wanted to be loved. People looked at me on the stage and they liked me. But they didn't know me. They accepted me for what I presented on stage, but that wasn't me. I was more than that. I wasn't sure what.

But I knew I had to find out.

Chapter Sixteen

It was almost like a dream. I had seen an old Robert Taylor movie once (with Brad, on "Party Night," while gulping Pepsi-floats and eating fudge) and in this movie Robert Taylor and a bus full of guys were packed into an army transport on some dangerous mission. I felt I was now living in that movie. The guys talked about how they were going to rip through this training business, get right on to the nitty-gritty, out there where it counts. *Counts.*

When the bus stopped, the door snapped open and a sergeant jumped on a step and screamed into the bus, "All right you goons, out! On the double!"

Then we boarded a plane to Fort Bliss, Texas. The guys were talking about wanting to be para-troopers, machine gunners, tank drivers; I didn't know what I wanted, except maybe to forget the whole thing, turn off the TV set and let Robert Taylor fade into a little white spot on the screen and vanish.

When we touched down, another sergeant bounded into the plane. "All right, move it! Get off this plane and get off now! Move it, dopey! On the double!"

The kid sitting next to me asked, "What is that man angry about?"

When he shouted "Atten-*tion!*" the place became a circus. Guys dropped things, froze on the spot, turned in circles; nobody knew where to look or how to stand. I couldn't help laughing. What a sorry group we were, the hope of the army!

It was cold and we complained miserably. I felt like a giant. My bunk was too short for me and there were no boots my size. "Man, are you serious? Dig this dude, man; he's got a size fourteen foot. Ain't nobody around here got a fourteen foot." They gave me the biggest size they could find.

Any man who has ever been in the service knows what that first trip to the barber is like. My hair was blond, over my ears, and carefully styled. When the sergeant called, "Fall in," I got to the end of the line so I could watch what happened to the other guys. I didn't want to be conspicuous. The sergeant saw me at the back and shouted, "About face!" I was first to get my haircut and suddenly became very conspicuous. The barber took one look at me and his eyes lit up with a sort of fiendish glee.

First he shaved a strip down the middle of my head, then, snickering with delight, shaved another strip. He cackled the whole time as if he were doing some work of art for the sake of a better mankind. When he was finished I looked like

Henry, the comic strip character. My only comfort was there were no girls around.

After a few weeks, platoon and squad leaders were designated and I was assigned to be a squad leader. I kept track of the guys in my squad, got them into formation, and reported to my platoon leader. Later I was assigned to be platoon leader and the squad leaders were reporting to me.

Every day there was inspection. Our foot lockers had to be hair perfect with soap, toothbrush, and comb in place. The beds had to be made as flat and straight as a plywood panel. We were told to make them so tight that a nickel dropped on them would bounce. At each weekly inspection, there were awards and ribbons for the top platoon. Mine was the top platoon for five weeks out of six. I figured out how to get the highest shine on our boots, taught the guys how to use pipe cleaners to get between the ridges of the brass; I showed them how to make the beds so the blankets looked as if they were painted on. When we lined up for inspection in the barracks I measured the men out so the space between them was perfectly even. Then I measured how far from the wall we should stand. Every bunk and every foot locker was measured in the same way.

I think the secret of our success was that I stressed working together. I placed real importance on the fact that if we argued, hassled each other, or didn't cooperate as a team, a unit, we'd never get anywhere. And we won the ribbons week after week.

I wrote to Xenia every day. The moments I spent

writing her were the highlight of the day.

By this time, I was thinking of becoming a Green Beret. Physically I was in good shape and the idea was a challenge. When I finished basic training I won the Outstanding Trainee trophy for my company. Then there was another award that was given to one man in the brigade. It was called the Spirit of Honor Medal for outstanding leadership. I won that award, too. It was hard for me to understand why I received those medals, when there were so many other guys who had just as much talent and ability.

Chapter Seventeen

Home on my first leave. Xenia didn't know what day I'd be arriving, so I paid a surprise visit to her parents' house in St. Paul. I was wearing my uniform, feeling very proud, as if I were somebody important, a person who had accomplished great things. The night was still, with large white snowflakes softly falling. I parked the car near the house by the corner street light and walked through the new-fallen snow to her front porch. It couldn't have been a more romantic setting.

I rang the bell and stood waiting at the front door. The chintz curtains in the window parted and Xenia's face appeared. I heard her scream, and then the door flung open and we were plunged into a love scene from a 1945 movie. I was the returning war hero and she was the beautiful and faithful girl friend back home.

The leave passed all too quickly and I was assigned to two weeks of special leadership training in Fort Lewis, Washington. I left Xenia and my family, and on New Year's Eve of 1966, I sat on a cold drafty train, puffing through the night air, feeling sorry for myself. The first eight weeks of basic training had been rigorous and rewarding but my army career hadn't even begun. I wondered what lay in wait for me in Fort Lewis.

"Well, Netherton," I said to the blank window, "Happy New Year."

I thought about a chapel service I had attended in Fort Bliss. A kindly looking woman with a brown ponytail stretched to the top of her head sang a song, "He's Everything to Me." I hummed the tune to myself now, unaware of the words.

I was in Leadership Preparation School in Fort Lewis before being sent to Advanced Infantry Training. Here we had classes, went out on maneuvers, marched, drilled, and were trained in leadership to fill in for noncommissioned officers who were serving in Vietnam.

Every day it rained. Sometimes we sat outside in the rain or snow for our classes. I'd worry about my feet being frostbitten while some sergeant was talking on about an M-16 rifle.

I wasn't even aware of the fact that Mount Rainier was within sight of the base, until one day when it stopped raining. It took me by surprise to see it there, magnificent, snow-peaked, rising up out of the mist like a glorious and majestic giant.

I figured there was a moral in its sudden appearance, something like, "Even though there's a sheet of rain covering everything, there's a magnificent mountain not far away—permanent, never mov-

ing. You may not be able to see it, but it's there."
That kind of thing. But I wasn't a philosopher or a
poet so I left it at that. I just knew I was impressed.

One of our classes was pugil stick training where
we learned hand-to-hand combat with rifles. Instead of the rifle we used pugil sticks with padding
on each end. The guys were eager to fight me because I was so big. We put on our helmets and
went at it like Robin Hood and Little John on their
first meeting. In the contests to see who could stay
on his feet the longest, I usually won. But one day I
was paired with an enormous Mexican fellow with
arms like tree trunks. He looked as if he was in the
ring to kill. We went at it with all our might. Just
when it looked as if I was going to win, another guy
jumped in the ring to help the Mexican! Cyrano de
Bergerac couldn't have fought more valiantly than
I. But finally one blow from the back sent me spin-
ning. I was unconscious standing up.

In the hospital I thought about the guys in my
platoon. Some of them couldn't even handle a
checkbook, others cried in their bunks at night.
And then there were the tough guys so filled with
anger and hate that they could hardly wait to get
hold of a gun and kill somebody.

I graduated Number Two in the class and was
made acting platoon sergeant during the rest of
my Advanced Infantry Training. Weeks later, I was
sent to Fort Benning, Georgia, to Officer Candidate School. Good old Fort Benning, where I had
lived as a child when my father was a major. There
was nothing nostalgic about it at all.

I saw the pine trees and the red clay earth from
the plane; all looked desolate, forlorn. March gray-

ness floated over it all. I arrived at the 84th Company Headquarters and stood for a moment outside the square, flat-roofed building. I went up the steps and reported in at the first sergeant's office. A clerk told me to wait.

While I was waiting, I saw a couple of guys in fatigues and tee shirts playing pool. I was watching them play when suddenly one of the men swung around and shouted, "What are you looking at, boy?" I straightened. "Well, what do you *think* I'm looking at?" Smart answer.

Not so smart. The man was a tactical training officer and I thought he'd go to pieces in front of me. He slapped the cue on the table, threw his arms in the air, and put his face right next to mine. "Who do you think you're talking to, boy? Do you know who I *am?*"

Another smart answer from me, twice as smart as the first one. "I don't know who you *are* and furthermore, I don't *care* who you are."

"I'm your commanding officer!"

The next thing I knew I was standing with my nose pressed against the wall and this second lieutenant was screaming at the top of his voice in my ear, *"Boy!* I am *personally* going to see that you don't get through this school! You stand against that wall with your nose pressing, you hear me, *pressing* the wall until I tell you to move, you got that, *boy?"*

I stood with my nose against the wall for three hours.

I could hear guys passing and commenting, "What'd he do?" "Whozzat?" "Did you see that poor slob candidate with his nose on the wall in there?"

We were usually up by 5:00 A.M. but many mornings it was 3:30 or 4:00. Our barracks were divided into small cubicles with two bunks and four desks in each cubicle. Four men shared these tiny spaces. Every morning at inspection the floors had to be spit-shined, every inch of space perfect. We had to be ingenious to meet these demands so we devised as many clever ways to do things as we could. When you have an 11:00 Lights Out and you were to be up at 4:00 A.M., you had to be ingenious. We had homework, classwork, drills, maneuvers, inspection, and it was impossible to do it all in the time you were allowed if you didn't work as a team, cooperating with each other and figuring out the fastest ways of doing things. Many nights we'd be spit-shining our boots and brass under our blankets with flashlights.

On the average we got three and a half to four hours of sleep a night, seven days a week. We could hardly stay awake in the classes in Infantry Hall during the day. One instructor would tell us, "Now I want you to know that anytime during this class, if I suddenly yell, 'Now!' you are to immediately jam your elbows into the guy on either side of you." Our uniforms were always fresh and crisp, but we didn't feel that way. Some of the guys sat in class with their eyes rolled up like window shades, others sat with their heads hanging over their books drooling. It was hilarious. Probably the only reason I didn't fall asleep is that I was laughing so hard at everyone else. I don't know how the instructors could stand to look at us.

I was exhausted all the time. I'm the kind of person who needs a lot of sleep. I have a theory that tall people need a lot of sleep. But I was determined to get through this thing and come out on top.

Our maneuvers usually had us out five to eight days in the thick forests and relentless rain. We were being prepared for Vietnam. We would spend days in the rain going through Georgian rivers and swamps, sleeping in water, eating in the water, never getting dry. One of the guys slipped into some mud up to his neck so he lived in wet mud for eight days; two of the other guys had jungle rot in their feet.

Most of the guys were tough and could take the pressure, but others just seemed to crumple under it. There was one man, an older guy, who agonized through every minute. I didn't see how you could get through OCS without at least some sense of humor. He just didn't have a bit of humor in him.

All of the candidates had their turn to be acting officers and one day I was Acting Company Commander. I marched my company back to the barracks and I saw my TAC officer with some of the other officers just coming out of the door. They were in their tee shirts and fatigues and were dirty and sweaty. It didn't look good.

I brought the company into the assembly area and yelled, "Left Face," so they would face me. I did an About Face to present the company to my TAC officer.

"Sir, Eighty-Fourth Company is ready for inspection."

He didn't say At Ease. He strolled around me, making a complete circle, slowly, deliberately, as I stood there in the dust at attention.

Then he said, "Candidate Netherton, do you know what a *blitz* is?"

When you spoke to an officer you had a special way of addressing him. "Candidate Netherton requests permission to speak, sir!"

"Speak!"

"No, sir!"

"Well, Candidate Netherton, we've had a little blitz today. Right in your company. Be ready for inspection at 2200 hours. *Dismissed!*"

We walked into the barracks and it was as if the place had been torn apart by tornadoes and floods and every disaster known to man. Shoes from the third floor were tangled with shoes from the first floor, beds were ripped up, furniture on end, sand, dirt, mud smeared everywhere. Clothes, blankets, belongings knotted together and thrown in piles on every floor and none of it belonging to that floor. The men, weary from marching all afternoon, stood in shock, their mouths agape.

Uniforms from the sixth platoon were tangled in uniforms from the third platoon; toothbrushes, shoelaces, socks, books, pencils so mixed up it would take a miracle to put it all back together again.

We had five hours.

I called the platoon leaders together and mapped out some strategy. I knew organization was the key, working together as a team. So we specialized. "Nelson, you're in charge of sheets. All sheets for every platoon. Machek, you've got shoes and shoelaces. Only shoes and shoelaces. And Dobbin, Larkoff, and Dennis, you've got beds. Just beds.

Get the beds," and that's how I narrowed it down.
That's how we worked.

At 2200 hours the company was standing at attention on gleaming spit-shined floors; everything
back in its place. That was the first time I ever saw
the TAC officer grin from ear to ear.

We had another horrendous event called Blue
Night. We would fall into bed at the end of the day,
muscles and nerves worn from the strain and
work, when all at once, without warning, a squad
of senior candidates wearing their gleaming blue
helmet liners would call us to attention and then
rush into the barracks, toss everything over, kick
the beds upside down, throw clothes, books, and
shoes in piles everywhere—and then order us all
outside for a two-mile run. We had to carry a
couple of the guys who collapsed.

We would have to be ready for inspection, clean
and spit-shined, first thing in the morning.

On some 2:00 A.M. occasions, we would be
awakened for a two-mile run, then brought back
on a low crawl across the parade field and training
field down into Raider Creek. Then we'd crawl
through the creek and stand at attention in the
cold until we did our PT exercises. After the exercises, we'd low crawl again, only this time through
the rocks, ripping our clothes up, and finally we
would be brought back double-time. We double-
timed right into the building, into our platoons,
and into our beds, muddy, wet, torn—covered
with dirt from our ears to our ankles.

We'd have to sweep, spit-shine, clean laundry
and clothes and be completely prepared for inspection at 5:30.

After inspection we had our classes. You can imagine what we must have looked like sitting in the quiet, stuffy rooms trying to keep awake.

All this to make leaders out of us.

Once I had accidentally left a postage stamp in the wrong place in my drawer. I had left it in a box of stationery and the TAC officer who inspected every inch of our quarters found it. I received a demerit for Failure to Secure Valuables. SOP, Standard Operating Procedures, had it that you had to secure valuables and my five-cent stamp was not secured. I had to write a 1,500-word theme, due the next day, on "Why I Failed to Secure My Valuables."

If you couldn't laugh at yourself you were in a sorry way, I'll tell you that.

News got around that I was a singer and the same TAC officer who had had me stand with my nose to the wall called me into his office one day after class. He sat back in his chair and put his spit-shined boots up on the desk.

"All right, Candidate Netherton, I hear you're a singer. So sing."

I responded. "Sir! Candidate Netherton requests permission to sing, sir!"

"Yeah, sing."

I gulped and began singing "The Shadow of Your Smile." He squinted his eye at me, as though I were making fun of him. "Are you singing that song to me?"

"Sir! Candidate Netherton requests permission to speak, sir."

"Speak."

"No, sir!"

"And why not?"

"Sir! You're too ugly, sir."

His feet fell from the desk. "I'm *what?*"

"Ugly, sir."

He pushed his chair back and pounded his fist on the desk. "Drop! Give me twenty!"

So I dropped and did twenty push-ups. And then twenty more. And twenty more.

That would not be the end of it. In the mess hall we had little time to eat and we had to eat "square meals"; that is, your hand had to go down into the food with your fork, straight up, and then make a 90° turn and straight across to your mouth. You were at attention the whole time, too, not looking at anyone else. If you accidentally let your eye slip to the side, an officer would shout, "You're eye-balling! Drop!" And you'd have to drop to the floor and do push-ups, or you would low crawl through the tables. You were also not allowed to talk. It was a good thing, because it was the hardest thing in the world to keep from laughing. We looked ridiculous.

I was eating one day, at attention, feet together, back upright, one-two-three with the fork, when I heard the familiar voice of my TAC officer shouting from the long table at the front of the mess hall, where the officers sat.

"Oh, Nether*ing*ton! Candidate Nether*ing*ton."

I knew he was talking to me but I wouldn't answer him until he pronounced my name correctly. He called me again in a laughing, sing-song voice. "Oh, Nether*ing*ton. . . ."

I went on eating one-two-three, ignoring him.

Time for basic training!

The guy next to me whispered through his teeth, "He's talking to you, man."

"That's not my name," I said, chewing a cooked carrot.

"Netherington!"

And he didn't even address me as "Candidate."

He was standing up now. Forks paused in midair. Every officer's eye was on me. "I see you,

119

Nethe*ring*ton! You hear me!" He came rushing
down off the platform and stood screaming in my
ear. "You're supposed to answer an officer when an
officer addresses you!"

I said, "Sir! Candidate Netherton requests permission to speak, sir."

"Speak!"

"Sir, my name is Candidate Netherton, not
Nethe*ring*ton. You were not calling me by name. If
you call me Candidate Netherton I will respond.
Nethe*ring*ton is not my name."

"Well, boy, I'm *making* it your name!"

"Sir! Candidate Netherton requests permission
to speak, sir."

"Speak!"

"Sir! You do not have legal authority to change
my name, sir."

He turned as red as a tomato. "I don't believe
this!" He stomped his foot and then shouted,
"Candidate *Netherton*, get up to the front of the
room!"

"Sir! Candidate Netherton requests permission
to go up to the front of the room, sir."

"Move it!"

The rest of the guys were snickering. He ordered
me to sing a song. I asked permission to speak
again and told him I couldn't do it without accompaniment. He shouted back, "I said sing!" I re-
quested permission to sing and started singing
"Moon River." The guys broke out in applause and
he screamed "Quiet!" They went on eating their
square one-two-three meals; I finished "Moon
River" and sang three more songs.

Chapter
Eighteen

From then on I had to sing every lunch hour. The TAC officer found a guy who played accordion, so he played and I sang. Some audience. Guys staring straight out ahead, sitting stiff in their seats, feet together, forks going one-two-three, no expression, just chewing and making squares with their forks.

I was on the sabre team and we performed for special occasions. We were a drill team and performed intricate maneuvers while precision marching and flipping the sabres. I was also on the Honor Guard. Being on the Honor Guard allowed me to guard for the Senior Blue Party. This is when the candidates reach the halfway mark of their training and receive blue epaulets, a blue helmet liner, and officer authority over the other candidates.

One of the guests was a perky girl who reminded me of the musical comedy performer Janis Paige.

She stood by me and although I wasn't allowed to talk, she talked to me. I had to stand at attention like a stone figure. Later I was given permission to join the party and I found her by the punch bowl. I liked her immediately and she liked me and gave me her telephone number. I had no idea she was my harassing TAC officer's girl friend.

When it came time for my own Blue Party I called her up and asked if she would be my date. She said she'd love to be. It was exciting to have a date after all the weeks of being with guys only. My TAC officer called me to his office. He was giving me instructions for the ceremony and then he said arrogantly, "You got a date, Netherton?"

I said, "Candidate Netherton requests permission to speak, sir," and told him yes I did have a date, sir.

He nodded with a sneer and said, "Oh, you do, huh? Hah! What's her name?"

I said, "Candidate Netherton requests permission to speak, sir," and told him her name. He turned blue, as if the oxygen in his body just left by way of his ears.

"What was that?"

I wondered if I had said something wrong and repeated her name. He slumped in his chair, grew small, shriveled. "That's all, Netherton," he said.

Later, the guys in the barracks told me she was his girl. We laughed at that—of all the girls in the world, how did I manage to pick my TAC officer's girl friend? The guys thought it was terrific.

"Man, oh, man, that's the best one yet!"

"Revenge is sweet, eh Tom?"

My parents drove down to Fort Benning for my

Blue Day. They drove my 1965 Cutlass convertible and left it there for me to use. When you were a senior candidate you were allowed to have a car. So there I was, stretched up taller than I ever had been, blue helmet and epaulets, ready to take life by the horns.

I had prayed more at OCS than I had in my entire life. My prayers were pleadings on the order of "Help!" I believed there was a heaven and hell and that if you were good you went to heaven; if you were bad you went to hell. But I didn't know what God considered good. I went on my own assumptions.

Now I was a Senior Candidate, a Blue. Now *I* was doing the shouting and the blitzing. I would roar into the new candidates' barracks and shout, "Attention!" The faces of the new candidates were pathetic with shock. One short fellow began to shake. "What's the matter with you?" I yelled. "Don't you know what to do when an officer walks in?" He stood at attention, still trembling.

"You know what you are, Candidate? You're gross. You are *gross*, Candidate."

I could hardly believe what I was doing. I began kicking over beds just as the officers before me had done. After the place was a national disaster area we left shouting, "Be ready for inspection at 5:30, got that?"

One of the candidates, fresh from boot camp, asked me one day if I would mind having my picture taken with one of the other candidates so he could send it home to his mother. He wanted a picture of me shouting at him.

"I don't believe you said that, Candidate!" I screamed. "Drop! Give me twenty!"

Then I made somebody else take a picture of him, instead of his friend. And I had them take it with me screaming in his ear, "You are the *worst*, Candidate."

My friends were stunned at the change in me, called me Dr. Jekyll and Mr. Hyde. I laughed, "You'll never make an officer if you don't act like one."

I knew how to be an officer. I had lived with one all my life.

But during the training I had moments of wanting to give up. There were men around me who cracked under the strain and did give up. Many of the guys who started OCS never finished. They couldn't take the exhaustion and stress.

The reasons I didn't quit were that I couldn't shame my parents and I knew Xenia would never understand. I told myself I wouldn't be a quitter, I'd just be eliminating a senseless torture. But I kept on.

And graduation day finally arrived. I had applied for Jump School and Special Forces (the Green Berets) and I expected to go to Vietnam. My career was laid out before me. My parents drove to Fort Benning for the graduation and it was a thrill to have my own father pin on my gold bars. I was now an officer in the United States Army. I was a second lieutenant.

I went home on leave and could hardly wait to see Xenia. I had written to her practically every day since I'd been away. Her picture on my desk had earned me harassment every time a TAC officer saw it. "Now what does a beautiful girl like that want with a nothing like you, Netherton?" I had gotten used to the insults. It was part of the training. When I became a senior candidate I drove the junior candidates nuts with harassing. And when they would graduate, they would understand, as I now did; it was all part of making soldiers out of civilians.

This soldier was eager to see his girl. I decided to show up at the Edgewater where she was still performing and surprise her. I dressed in my officer's uniform and drove to the club.

I was flushed with excitement as I shook hands with the maitre d', but he seemed somewhat reserved. I didn't notice it in my eagerness to surprise Xenia. Inside, sitting ringside, were her parents. I rushed to join them, expecting joyful surprise. But their reaction to their would-be-son-in-law was strained, awkward. I paid no attention. I was so eager to fix my eyes on Xenia again. She came out on stage looking gorgeous and she sang beautifully—until she saw me. Then her performance fell apart. She fumbled, stumbled, lost her place in the music, her voice cracked, she forgot words. I thought maybe I should have telephoned her first—she was so overcome with happiness at the sight of me.

After the show, when I kissed her, I knew immediately something was wrong.

"Things have changed," she told me in a strained voice.

"Changed?"

"I've been seeing someone else. You see, Tom, you were gone and I needed someone. It's hard to be alone, Tom. I needed someone."

I couldn't believe what I was hearing.

"Please understand, it's just that I couldn't be alone. You weren't here—I needed someone. I'm going to marry him."

And she did.

Chapter Nineteen

I waited for my orders for Vietnam. The obstacle courses we had had during training would be real then: real machine guns, machetes, grenades and bombs exploding, and trenches and foxholes dug in putrid swamps—the real thing; no longer simulated battle situations.

I was aware of the anti-Vietnam demonstrations across the U.S. and of the draft card burnings, and I knew what a demoralizing effect it had on the GIs over there rotting in the swamps. By 1967, 389,000 American soldiers were in Vietnam.

"It's not civil responsibility the draft dodgers and deserters are concerned with," my father said emotionally. "It's their interest in saving their own skins."

I thought about dying. My one worry was that my life would not have counted for anything. I still thought of the faces of the Indians in Peru. I thought of the guys in basic training, crying in physical and mental agony at night. And I felt helpless.

But when my orders came, they were for Panama, not Vietnam. I reasoned I would be going to jungle warfare school, and then to Vietnam, I hoped, with the Green Berets.

I arrived in Panama City in a torrent of rain. It rained almost every afternoon from about May to October during *invierno,* or winter season. But when the rain stopped, the early evening was beautiful with sky meeting oceans on both sides of the land, and the smells of salt water and tropical trees and foliage.

Panama City was a modern, progressive city with tall white buildings, American companies, billboards, and skyscrapers. American and European cars moved along the streets. At rush hour, the streets were more congested than downtown Los Angeles. I was sent to Fort Clayton and assigned as an infantry officer in a mechanized battalion.

One of my duties was to be up at 5:30 in the morning and help lead the men in PT exercises. The training officers had to do the exercises with the men and were supposed to make it look easy. We took them on two-mile runs shouting orders and always keeping our knees higher and our steps lighter than theirs. When they were exhausted, we were supposed to keep going with the energy of a jeep. We weren't even supposed to breathe hard. I had turned into a real-life Superman, at least while in front of them. But when we reached our quarters and were out of sight, we too collapsed in pools of sweaty exhaustion.

We went on maneuvers into the steaming jungles where we'd be dropped at a certain spot and then required to find our way back alone. On our first maneuver of this type, we were heading for a bivouac site in a snag of trees the first night, but hanging right in the center of our twisting trail was a boa constrictor. It was the kind you'd hope to see safely curled behind a glass wall at the Bronx Zoo. It was a fat thing with a head the size of a large zucchini squash.

I ordered the men to pass it one at a time, quickly. One of the men was so terrified he missed his footing and became entangled in the vines right beneath the swaying head of the snake. He nearly passed out in fear. I tried to coax him gently through and, for a few minutes, wondered if he'd make it.

He did, we all did, and we bedded down for the night in the dampness among the large brown ants which we could hardly avoid no matter how carefully we shook out our bedrolls.

One of the men let his hand drop out onto the ground as he slept. It fell on a brown ants' nest. In the morning his hand was swollen and red and I had to call in Air Support for a helicopter to come and take him out of the jungle for medical help.

Each day the jungle looked different to me; the rivers twisted in different directions and there were never any landmarks or blazed trails. It was always hot, humid, a mass of vines and impossible tangles.

My platoon sergeant and I took the men through rivers, wading in mud and slime up to our chins, making our way to the battalion rendezvous point.

These maneuvers were a test for me as well as for the men, like Hannibal crossing the Alps. Although wet and weary, we were glad to be the first platoon to make it to the rendezvous point. As a green lieutenant, I was just glad that I had the help of a seasoned platoon sergeant.

I also had to learn how to operate an armored personnel carrier. Although the young officers had textbook knowledge of personnel carriers from OCS, we had to learn how to operate them as well. We sat on the high metal stools inside with only our heads poking out the hatches and roared through the jungles. I learned how to handle these thirteen-ton monsters as easily as my '65 Olds Cutlass, maybe better.

The day I received my final orders, I was sitting at the officers' club with some of the other officers who were expecting to go to Vietnam. The orders had been changed; I wasn't going to join the Green Berets, wasn't going to Vietnam—my orders said two years in Panama.

Wearing my uniform that was so starched I could hardly get my foot into the pants, I looked out over the palm trees brushing their long green fingers in the breeze and saw the twinkling lights of Panama City reflected in the bay. I had a dramatic sense of something supernatural going on that I wasn't aware of.

Lighting a cigarette, I leaned back against the stone wall of the patio. For the first time, I felt that maybe my life would count for something after all. I had the strongest sensation I was in Panama for a purpose.

I had begun to smoke a little and to drink. After all, that is what officers were expected to do. I was not blasé about my men, though. I really cared about them. I was tough and could shout orders louder than anybody you've ever heard, but they knew I wasn't a punk lieutenant taking out my own personal hostilities on them. I sat up many nights counseling and giving advice. I was a combination bartender - psychologist - baby - sitter - social - worker - and - parole - officer.

But I wasn't sure how much help I really was. You can say a lot of good things but they don't always have the power to give real help to a guy when he's in trouble or actually to change his life for the better.

When I learned that I wasn't going to join the Green Berets in Vietnam after all, I was disappointed and relieved at the same time. I had been so geared for Nam; everything we did in training and OCS was aimed toward going there.

One of the social centers for the young officers was our Officers' Club Beach. I began spending free time on the clean, warm sand there as well as at Taboga Island surrounded by leafy pineapple plants and 400-year-old tamarind trees. It took me a while to adjust to the fact that I was really here in this tropical paradise that was once one of the richest and most luxurious havens in the world.

One evening when I was having a drink at the Officers' Club, a first lieutenant who lived at the BOQ (Bachelor Officers' Quarters) invited me to a Bible study. The idea sounded somehow out of place. But I went. Then I began attending the services at the Christian Servicemen's Center. The fellow who ran it was a dynamic man, outgoing and loving. His wife was a warm and friendly woman who served home-cooked meals for the guys on Sundays.

I began to read the Bible from time to time on my own. ". . . My son, give me your heart. . . ."

I began singing at the piano bar of the Officers' Club in Fort Kobbe, too. The new interim commanding officer, Lt. Col. Morrissey of our battalion, was there one night with his wife, Marie, and we sat and talked.

The next day I was called to his office. I thought I had done something wrong. But he told me that the Inspector General for South America had a daughter who needed an escort to a military function and would I consent to being her escort? I said, "Yes, sir!" A couple of weeks later when Col. Morrissey went back to his brigade command, I was transferred to brigade level as the Assistant Plans Operations Officer. I would be working at the 193rd Brigade Headquarters now.

There had been riots a couple of years ago in the Canal Zone and things looked bad because of the upcoming Panamanian elections. I was in charge of certain emergency plans concerning Latin America, under the supervision of the Colonel. I met with the Panamanian National Guard, representatives of the Canal Zone and Panamanian governments, and various U.S. military agencies to finalize a plan for Panama. The day I was to brief General Johnson on the new plan, I was more nervous than on an opening night. Top secret security clearance . . . armed guards outside the briefing room. I felt like James Bond.

During this time I was still singing at night on off-duty hours and I was invited to sing with the Army and Air Force Bands. I made several appearances with them and began singing on the Southern Command Television Network in Panama, too. With my car, headquarters job, and Foster Grant sunglasses, I felt like a pretty groovy dude. Life was just a bowl of mangoes.

Except there was still this strange feeling inside me that I was in Panama for some important purpose and I knew I hadn't found it yet.

I went snorkeling and skin diving off Taboga Island, dancing at the Hilton, and partying on the beaches with the cream of Panamanian society, but there was a longing, a deep longing, going far beyond the tropical nights and days. Nothing seemed to satisfy it. It had been there all my life.

Chapter Twenty

Occasionally I attended the Bible studies at the First Baptist Church. One day a friend of mine, Lieutenant Fred Dickerman, asked if I'd like to hear Major Ian Thomas at the church. I had never heard of Major Thomas, but I didn't have anything else to do, so I went along with him.

During the service I sensed that something strange was beginning to happen to me. For the first time in my life the words about Jesus made sense; the message was rich with love and power. As I sat there among all those strangers, I suddenly felt a surge of expectation.

All at once I felt a tingling go through my body, as it had once before when I was a child—it was the same sensation—as though God was touching me, breathing on me.

"Lord, I've got to know for sure who you are and whether all this that I'm hearing is true. I've got to know! I know you're the Creator but I don't know what else you are. If you can show me tonight that Jesus is real, then I will give my life to him."

There was no voice from heaven. No bolt of lightning. No thunder. But I sat amid those people, none of them knowing what was happening to me, and I met my Savior.

At once I knew he was real, that as the Son of God, he gave his life for me, for the whole world. I knew that moment that by giving my life to him, I would be empowered by the Holy Spirit to be the kind of man God had always intended for me to be. Everything became clear to me, as clear as the pure Panamanian rain waters that washed everything clean.

"Take my life," I whispered, "and use it any way you want to. Jesus, I give myself to you."

There was an altar call but I didn't go forward. My friend, who didn't know anything of the dramatic event taking place at his side, was disappointed that I stayed in my seat. He knew how desperately I needed the Lord and he wanted very much for me to find him.

I felt something within me saying to wait until tomorrow night. I'd have my chance to make a public stand then.

The next night the Billy Graham film *The Restless Ones* opened, and I was supposed to be one of the counselors. It was a ridiculous idea, because I didn't know a thing to tell anyone, except now I knew that God was real and that I had given my life to him.

At the close of the film Dr. Graham gave his invitation for those who wanted to give their lives to the Lord. He told us to go to the front of the theater where counselors would be waiting to pray with us.

I sat there motionless. It was an intimidating notion. What if some of my men were there? What if they laughed at me? And besides, I was so tall everybody would notice me. There was no way to go unnoticed.

But then I told myself, "I have just met the God of the universe. I want people to know that. I want the whole world to know!" and I got out of my seat and rushed down the aisle. I was the first one to go forward.

The Christians from the Bible study and the church were so excited they hugged me and whooped, "Praise God!" And my friend who brought me was so moved he could hardly speak. He knew how miserable my life was, even though outwardly I appeared to have the world by the tail.

That was the trouble. I had been basically a good person all my life. I didn't see my need for a Savior. I didn't know that my life was ugly in sin because I never did anything that seemed to be really ugly. I had never really done anything with intentions to hurt anyone. I was a "good" person. In fact, since I was ten years old, I had heard people say things like, "Tom is so nice—so *responsible.*"

That was just it! I had been trying to live a good life, doing good, being good, in order to gain the self-worth and value everyone craves. But that isn't what God has planned for people at all. His plan is that we give our lives to him and then he, by the power of the Holy Spirit, gives us in return, strength, energy, ability, talent, and power to become like him.

I realized that in Christ I would find my real self. I wanted him to control every detail of my life.

I began to enjoy reading the Bible; if I started reading at six o'clock in the evening I would still be sitting in the same position, as though pasted to the pages, at midnight. The Officers' Club, the drinking, the partying, and cruising around town in my car didn't have the same attraction anymore.

The Word of God at last made sense. It all fit together. Every word was alive, real. I understood why the Bible says that a person has to be spiritual in order to understand spiritual things. Now the words were important, and I was uncontrollably excited, as though I had come in contact with life for the first time.

Chapter
Twenty-One

I began to pray for a job that would give me weekends free so I could attend church regularly. I wanted to be with Christians and to go to their meetings. God answered my prayer and I received a new position as Entertainment Officer. This new job meant working in the field I enjoyed most; besides, I had weekends free. I moved into an apartment off-base with my friend Fred Dickerman.

We would take long walks along the *Plaza de Francia*, through Old Panama City, and along beautiful *Via España* and talk about the Lord. I wanted to know about denominations, ministries, and what it meant to be a Christian. I was sure that the greatest event of my life was giving my life to Jesus Christ. It had happened in Panama—my premonitions had been right when I felt something great would happen to me here.

I began dating a beautiful Panamanian Christian girl named Yolanda and we formed a singing group with one of our friends, Steve Bolt. Our little trio sang every week at churches and different functions around the Zone. I had never been happier. When the United States sent Apollo 8 into moon orbit I was orbiting in the heavenly spheres with Jesus.

Many changes took place in my life when I gave it to the Lord; everything around me looked brighter, better. Colors seemed more vibrant; music sounded sweeter, and food tasted better. At one time I didn't care for the Panamanian food, but now *arróz con camarones* washed down with ice cold guava juice thoroughly delighted me. I felt free from past dislikes, fears, and, best of all, free from the haunting worry that my life wouldn't count for anything. My life now belonged to Jesus and it was his to do with as he wanted. I trusted him completely.

It was in Panama I first learned of denominational hassles among Christians. I was surprised that Christians would find fault with each other or separate into cliques. We are all born-again people, walking with the power of the Holy Spirit in our lives. It seems ridiculous to separate over issues that have little relevance to the gospel of Christ at all.

But I learned that Christians are people, people who need to learn how to follow the ways of love. Some of them never do, and that's too bad.

I made a decision early in my Christian walk. I decided not to look at Christians in order to learn about heaven, but to look to the Lord. That way I would love people, especially God's people, without expecting them to be perfect and flawless.

My letters home were brimming with the exciting news of my conversion. I wrote pages of my testimony to my family and included pleas for them to give their hearts to God as I had done.

I received loving letters in return but there was no mention of Jesus.

When I was snorkeling off Taboga Island one day, I was praying about my future and asking the Lord to show me his will for my life. I realized suddenly that I had gone out a little too far and was separated from my diving party. The current was very strong and I began to wrestle against it. I wasn't having any success and I felt a cold hand of fear grab my chest.

"Lord! I'm losing control."

At that moment I looked up and saw coming at me what appeared to be the biggest whale I'd ever seen. It was streaking toward me at high speed, silver and glimmering in the reflection of the sun in the water. As it grew closer, I panicked. There was nothing I could do. To dive deeper would have been pointless. As the giant thing came upon me, it broke into millions of silver lights, everywhere, brilliant, jewel-like, shimmering, and I saw I was completely engulfed in fish—glittering silver fish, like an enormous underwater fireworks. I swam with them in the blaze of silver and then as abruptly as they had appeared, they were gone.

Back on shore I knelt in the sand and told the Lord that for the rest of my days I would live to serve him.

It was nearly time for me to return to the States. Some of my friends were telling me that singing in nightclubs was wrong. I answered them firmly and resolutely, "Whatever I do, I do for the Lord. Whether I sing in a nightclub or dig trenches in swamps; it makes no difference. I do it all for him. My life is his." But I was beginning to think about becoming a foreign missionary.

I arrived back in the States in August of 1969. I was happy to be home and could hardly wait to tell people about my new life as a Christian. I preached relentlessly to anyone who had ears, and my family was my main target. One afternoon I was "preaching" to my mom as she was stirring up the batter for Danish coffee cake. Finally she stopped and said, "Tom, that's enough."

"Pardon me?"

"I said, that's enough. I have my religion and you have yours. Now yours is fine for you and I'm really happy for you, but I want you to leave the rest of us alone."

"But, Mom, I'm only sharing the Good News!"

"Your Good News is driving us bananas."

I decided not to be the family evangelist anymore. Instead, I prayed for each of them quietly, alone, where they couldn't see or hear me.

I went to work at Poulliot Design Company, a maker of artificial plants and trees, in Edina. I worked drilling holes in dried twigs, plugging them with leaves, and then dipping them into boiling wax to make Christmas decorations. Here I was, an army officer who had once worked on top secret government plans with armed guards around me, now making $2.50 an hour gluing twigs together.

I had told the Lord on the beach that day in Panama I would serve him all the days of my life and I meant that promise. So I glued and dipped leaves in wax, hoping for better things later on.

At home, my sisters and brother were involved with school activities and with their friends. Brad was captain and president of everything possible, Julie was on the dance team and cheerleading, and Wendy was Miss Congeniality of the known world. They had many friends and were usually out with them. It was my parents I was concerned about. I rarely saw them laughing or touching these days. My father's dark moods were more and more frequent. My mother began retreating to her room in cold silences, unlike her. Her usual bubbly personality gave way to periods of sullenness and brooding.

After a while I changed jobs and went to work at Peterson's Shoes in Minnetonka as a shoe salesman. Selling shoes was a tiring job, but I had promised the Lord that everything I did was for him, so I sold shoes for the glory of the Lord.

"I asked for red, not brown."

"Yes, ma'am. I'll get them for you."

"I changed my mind. I'll see the brown."

"Yes, ma'am. I'll get them for you."

"I think I like the red better."

"Did you want to take the red, then?"

"Do you have them in navy?"

"Yes, ma'am. I'll get them for you."

"I changed my mind. I'll see them in black."

"Yes, ma'am. I'll get them for you."

"I like them in black."

"Did you want to take the black, then?"

"I don't think so. How about that style over there? Do you have those in red?"

As I worked I prayed for my parents. I knew that if God's love got through to their hearts, a miracle could happen between them. But a miracle didn't happen.

After a year, with a little money in the bank, I put my last box of shoes on the shelf, brought out the last pair to a customer, and said good-bye to selling shoes. I decided to go to a Bible school for missionary training to prepare for service in Latin America.

"But why a foreign missionary? Can't you convert lost souls here in your own country? I mean, there are lots of sinners here. Just look around you—we have lots of sinners right here in Bloomington."

"Mom, I want to be a foreign missionary."

"Well, you could be a local missionary, couldn't you? Think of that, why don't you?"

"I've made my decision."

I applied and was accepted at Bethany Fellowship Missionary Training Center in Bloomington. I was packing to leave for Bible school, putting my new Andraé Crouch record into the suitcase, when Mom came into my room and stood at the doorway watching me. She had a sweet glow on her face.

"Tom?" She was hesitant, but then she said softly, "I understand now."

"Understand?" I thought maybe she was talking about the clutter on my bed.

"Yes. About your decision. About your new life. I've given my life to Christ, too." I couldn't help crying as I hugged her.

Again, a few days later, I found myself misty-eyed as my sister Julie stood at my doorway and told me the same thing. Then, before I left for school, Brad and I sat up late talking long after everyone else had gone to bed. Later that week he bowed his head and asked Christ to come into his heart.

There was more joy in store for me when on one sunny afternoon my youngest sister, Wendy, gave her heart to the Lord. It's hard to describe how happy we all were. Now we could go to church together with new excitement in our hearts, with new life, with God's love filling us and drawing us to him and to each other.

I had always felt close to my brother and sisters, mainly because I always thought they were wonderful people. But now there was an extra special bond, and I enjoyed more than ever my involvement in their lives. Julie and I became even closer than before. She was at a dating age and would come into my room after a date and sit on the edge of the bed and tell me all about the events of the evening.

Wendy was growing into a fine young lady and had so much enthusiasm and energy. Being a part of her life was always an adventure. And how I enjoyed Brad, for he was no longer just a brother, but my best friend.

It was a warm September morning when I left for Bible school, the kind of day when Minnesotans sit outside their houses on lawn chairs; they walk instead of taking their cars, and barbecue on their patios in a last outdoor fling before the onset of winter. Winters are long in Minnesota and the summers far too short. If it's a mild September, Minnesota folk say they're having a hot spell.

I especially noticed the weather that morning because the streets, the lawns, the sky, the trees, even the bicycles and cars in the driveways were covered with a film of bright morning dew and everything I saw looked silver and shining, as though touched by God.

Chapter
Twenty-Two

Life at Bethany Fellowship Missionary Training Center was difficult for me at first. After having been a professional entertainer, an officer in the army, and having seen other parts of the world, I was now living with young people just out of high school. I was on a curfew and not allowed to date.

But I was eager to please the Lord. It was the Lord I wanted to be close to and know with my heart and soul. I believed that the teachers and leaders of the school were there to show me how to live and serve the Lord. I trusted them and believed their rules and regulations were for my good.

We had classes in the morning and then in the afternoons we worked in the trailer factory where the students helped build Bethany campers. This was the business that supported the school. Instead of paying high tuition, we were able to work for our board and room and partial tuition.

There, among the students on the campus, I realized how deep my need for Christ had been all my life. I saw myself back at Bloomington High doing all of the right things, being the perpetual Nice Guy so people would like me. My own reputation and popularity had been more important to me than anything.

One Wednesday night in chapel, I sat with the other students listening to Pastor Hegre preaching. Right in the middle of the sermon he stopped and said, "I feel the Lord wants me to stop here." We all sat up straighter in our seats. It was an unusual thing for him to stop right in the middle of preaching. I'd never heard anyone do that before. Then he said, "I feel God wants me to stop preaching and take the rest of this time for each one of us to ask the Holy Spirit to help us love Jesus more."

Talk to the Holy Spirit? Well, why not? He is the third member of the Godhead. I talk to God and to Jesus. I should talk to the Holy Spirit, too.

Pastor Hegre continued. "Jesus loves us deeply and he longs for his children to love him back. He yearns for us to love him in a deeper way. Only the Holy Spirit can give us that kind of love."

I heard a muffled sob behind me. Then the student sitting next to me began sniffling and pulling tissues out of her purse. I felt the presence of the Holy Spirit sweep across the auditorium. The entire student body began praying, some weeping, some on their knees, some with their hands in the air.

The Holy Spirit was so near, so real, that I strongly sensed his love and power. The tears streamed down my face. I prayed and wept shamelessly as I realized what the Lord had done for me. I knew this was more than just an emotional experience. I realized anew how much the Lord wanted me to love him.

I wept long after the service was over. I couldn't stop. I went downstairs to the choir rehearsal room and stayed there alone, praying and weeping. Then late in the night I had an experience I shall never forget. It was something I saw—not a supernatural vision, but a kind of picture in my own head, bright and alive. I saw Jesus in my mind, and he had his dear arms outstretched to me. His arms, his presence then embraced me— engulfed me as the school of silver fish had in the water off Taboga Beach. His presence was everywhere, in every inch of space. Then I imagined him saying, with the voice that sang the original love song, "My son, you have given me your heart." I felt wonderfully and truly loved.

Chapter
Twenty-Three

I concentrated on my studies with eagerness to learn all I could about the Lord. In class I drank in the words of my teachers, taking notes, and trying to swallow in gulps the great truths I was learning. I received good grades in most of my classes but the spiritual wealth placed in my heart far exceeded any grades I could have earned.

Each year there was a special Christmas program presented by the students, and I was made chairman for that year's program. I worked hard at it, forming trios and quartets of singers, working on staging, selecting music and costumes, and designing the sets. I had some special lighting brought in and I was a veritable Cecil B. DeMille of the campus.

I don't know if you can call a Christmas pageant a hit, but ours was just that. The students thought it was terrific. The faculty was less enthusiastic, however. They worried about the production being too worldly. I was surprised at their reaction.

I began singing in several of the school programs. I was eager to perform for the Lord and sing
the songs I loved most to sing, songs about him
and his love. One day I was called into the counselor's office.

"Tom, there's been a bit of dissension."

"There has?" I didn't know what he was talking
about.

"Yes. Your singing is a little bit too worldly for
the church."

"Too worldly? How can that be?"

"Well, Tom, you *croon*. And another thing, you
hold the microphone in your hand the way a night
club entertainer would."

"Sir, I'm sorry if I have offended anyone, but the
way I sing is the way I express myself."

"Well, if you could change your style—"

"But I sing from my heart."

I respected my teachers and counselors and I
was disturbed by this admonition. I wanted to
please the Lord. If I wasn't pleasing him with my
singing, then maybe I shouldn't be doing it.

I was transferred from working on the camper
assembly line to the outside crew where I did jobs
such as cleaning, repairing, and maintaining the
grounds. My co-worker, Paul Madison, and I were
assigned to paint a fence behind the publication
building one afternoon. It started out circum-
spectly enough, but then I accidentally spattered a
little paint on him. He, in return, splashed a dollop
of white on me. I turned and sprayed him in polka
dots. He dipped into the bucket and sent a shower

flying at me. I attacked with the brush. He coun-
terattacked with his. Then we grabbed the rollers
and rolled stripes of white across each other. We
were laughing and yelling, and we finished painting the fence like Laurel and Hardy in one of their
improbable comedies.

Then the lunch bell sounded. We hurried to the
cafeteria, unaware of the shock we must have
caused. We sat down to eat our baked chicken and
home fries when the loudspeaker clicked on. An
announcement was made that anyone who was
covered in paint should not eat in the cafeteria.

I did some crazy things with the other students
like short-sheeting the teachers' beds when they
were at a faculty banquet, or sneaking girls into
the boys' dorm to show off the way we had fixed up
our rooms. One day, just as some girls got up the
stairs, the monitor came by. We quickly stashed
them in the closets. I had a camera, and after the
monitor left, I took a picture of the girls poking
their heads out of the closet. I laughed and teased
that I now had evidence for blackmail. Then I
shouted, "Monitor!" and the girls stumbled into
the closets again, alarmed. The third time I yelled
"Monitor," they knew I was kidding and fled the
dorm so quickly, you would have thought a swarm
of hornets was after them.

We worked hard keeping the dorm clean, although most of the guys didn't like cleaning. But
every once in a while we'd have an all-out, rip-
roaring shaving cream fight. The place would be
buried in white foam and then we'd have to work
twice as hard cleaning up.

I didn't mind being a clown. I often thought how simple life was when lived for God. The most simple things can be exciting and wonderful. I gained new appreciation for little things. I appreciated the fun we had and I also appreciated things like conversation.

One night a group of us went to hear Paul Stookey who at one time sang with Peter, Paul, and Mary. He was now a radiant Christian and I was thrilled listening to him sing and speak. I felt a twinge of longing in my own heart to sing again.

That longing began growing stronger. I braved singing for some of our programs but once again I was called into the counselor's office. "You're crooning again, Tom."

I began to wonder if I was meant to be a missionary after all.

Now I began to rebel. I didn't think the faculty understood me and I decided to leave school. But the Lord wouldn't allow me to leave. My attitude was negative and selfish.

"But, Lord," I tried to reason with him, "they think I'm *worldly.*"

When I finally began to date, I took one of the students, Joni Berger, out. We went to Christian concerts and had long talks together. Joni was a slim blonde girl with a compassionate and sweet personality. We began a long and lasting friendship.

"Joni, I don't understand it. Nobody sees my point of view. I think one way, but the school thinks another."

"There's nothing wrong with Christians holding different opinions, is there?" she'd tell me. "—That is, if the essentials are agreed on."

Rebellion, bitterness, hurt—all welled up within me. How could I get along at a school where my ideas were considered so radical? I wanted to sing, produce lively, bright shows—they said I was worldly.

But then, in time, I began to see that it is possible to love and respect people even if their ideas are different from mine. I needed to put aside my need for acceptance and appreciate the people around me for who they were, not for what I wanted them to be.

I learned to gain a love for my teachers and for the school, in spite of our differences. I realized what they stood for and how deep their commitment to Jesus was.

My friends didn't want me to leave school because of the fun we had and the student life we shared, but I felt that leaving was the right thing to do. The people at the school would remain my friends, but I felt the Lord was moving me on.

I had been at school a year and a half when I made the decision to leave. I had been praying about singing again and it became almost my only thought. Day and night I thought about arrangements, instruments, songs. I thought about singing more than I did about my studies.

My father was even more disgruntled than the counselors at school. "Quitting? First you want to be a missionary and now you want to go back to singing. Do you really know what you want?"

Those last words hit me hard. I felt the familiar

old curse I had lived and slept with my whole life before I met the Lord—would I ever really amount to anything?

Again I prayed. "Don't let me do the wrong thing, Lord. Show me your will."

I called a local theatrical agency and asked if there was an opening in a show for me. I knew my motivation for returning to show business was right. I wasn't seeking self-esteem or identity any more. I wasn't looking for acceptance and the praise of other people. My goal was to bring people to Jesus.

I asked the Lord to show me whether I was doing the right thing. I believed he answered me when the agency called with an opening for me to sing with the Lamplighters, a popular singing group at McGuire's Supper Club in St. Paul.

My instructors and counselors were sorry to see me leave, but I knew that they wanted the Lord's will for my life as much as I did. I realized if I wasn't supposed to be a missionary it would be wrong for me to be one, even if I accomplished wonderful things at it. I thanked them for all they had done for me and for their loving help in my life.

One of my instructors said to me, with damp eyes. "We all love you, Tom, and we're cheering for you."

"I love you, too," I said. And I meant it.

Chapter Twenty-Four

It felt good to be performing again. I began to pray for people in the audiences, something I would continue to do throughout my career. An audience was now more than just a sea of faces in the darkness. I saw the people as individuals and each one important.

I sang at McGuire's Supper Club and then with a new group at the Camelot Restaurant in Bloomington.

My brother, Brad, had been dating a beautiful girl named Jennifer since they were both in high school. On January 8, 1972, they were married. I sang at the wedding. They made a great couple and I was very proud of them. It gave me a special feeling of joy to see Brad so happy.

Our show at the Camelot prepared us for a booking in Chicago at the Arlington Towers Hotel, which would become the Arlington Hilton. It was a luxury hotel with a lovely supper club at the top. We opened at the Arlington for a two-week run. We were extended for three weeks. Then six; twelve. In all, we were there nine months.

We performed two shows a night and three on Saturdays. It was hard work, but in that time I learned hundreds of songs and gained valuable experience in singing and dancing.

I spent many days in Chicago with our friends the Whitesells. Doris Whitesell had been my mother's best friend for many years, and her children were the same age as the children in our family. I felt right at home in their Chicago house on Pensacola Avenue. Just being in their home was a happy, loving experience. And the Whitesells were my biggest fans.

"The wonderful thing about you," Doris told me once, her bright blue eyes sparkling, "is that you are so—so down to earth."

That surprised me.

"Yes, you aren't vain and stuck on yourself, Tom. Even though you are a show business personality now, you haven't lost any of the everyday qualities you had as a child growing up."

I laughed. "But I've never considered myself anything other than 'down to earth.' " I was certain that if the Lord ever permitted me to know great success in show business it would be as a down to earth person.

At the Arlington, the director gave me a song at rehearsal one day that I knew I couldn't sing. I objected to the words.

"What do you mean you can't do the number? What's wrong with it? It's a harmless number."

"I don't care for the lyrics. I can't sing a song like this. It's just not the kind of song I can sing."

My brother Brad and his wife Jennifer.

"Ah! I get it. It's the swearing, right? You object to the swearing."

"Right."

"For crying out loud. Tom, you know what? You are really weird."

But they changed the number.

We began accumulating a stack of excellent reviews. The Chicago *Tribune* said, "Tom Netherton is a great talent. He's destined to be a star on the major cafe circuit." I was encouraged by these reviews, to say the least.

All the kids in the show got along well together. It was interesting to me to discover they thought I was religious, but a nice guy in spite of it. I wondered why the word *religious* had such a bad connotation.

Maybe it's because *religious* doesn't necessarily mean *kind* or *compassionate.* I prayed that the Lord would never let me forget that I was, as Doris Whitesell had told me, a "down to earth person," and that applied to my Christianity, too. Christians care about other people and put God first in their lives. That's the kind of person I wanted to be. Nothing less.

I attended Rolling Meadows Baptist Church and met many wonderful Christians. Their prayers and support encouraged me more than the reviews and audience response.

The group I was performing with disbanded and I was asked to join a Las Vegas-type show to play the Chicago clubs. I objected to much of the material and didn't care for the comedian they hired. The show just wasn't my style. I tried to explain that the way I wanted to express myself was not in blue humor or sexy numbers.

"Besides, I believe in encouraging a moral life, not downgrading it. Doing risqué material is demoralizing. I won't do it."

So I was once again without a job. My friends at Rolling Meadows as well as the pastor, Michael Green, were prodding me to go out on my own as a solo gospel singer. They insisted churches all over the country would be just delighted to pay me to come and sing for them. It sounded good, and with their enthusiastic urging as well as financial support to buy a van and sound equipment, supplied by some other dear friends, the Paices, I set off to become the gospel performer of the highways and byways of Christendom.

Disaster!

The first church I sang at paid me $25.00 and that didn't even cover the gas to get there. I hired an accompanist to play for me, and when I received $15.00 for the concert, I paid her and had to borrow money to buy myself a hamburger.

For some churches to pay anything at all was a sacrifice on their parts. (In fact, some of the churches expected one to sing for free because it was supposed to be "unto the Lord and not for filthy lucre.") At last, when I couldn't manage any longer, I went back home to Bloomington. I was weary, depressed, and defeated as I drove up the short driveway to my mom's house.

My spiritual life began a swift decline. I began to wonder if I had made a mistake leaving Bible school. I wondered if I was really in God's will. I didn't have a supper club job and now I realized the churches didn't want me, either. Eventually, I wondered if God was truly with me at all.

I hadn't learned how to thank him in all things, and because I'd never been in such dismal circumstances since becoming a Christian, I reacted selfishly.

Other guys my age had careers or college degrees or at least wives. I had none of these. "I'll never amount to anything," I grumbled.

Things weren't that bubbly at home either. My parents had now gotten a divorce. My dad had moved out to an apartment and my mom was working in an office after twenty-six years of being a homemaker.

Every day after my mom left for work I would wander around the house trying to think of things to do. There were no singing openings and no other job openings either. (I didn't want to go back to selling shoes!) My thinking was clouded by self-pity and anger. I couldn't figure out why God had allowed me to fail so miserably. After all, I had earnestly wanted to serve him, hadn't I?

I decided to sell real estate. After getting my license I went to work selling houses. From the time I entered the real estate business until I left, I did not sell one house.

The days turned to weeks, the weeks to months. Summer came and went; autumn drifted by; the cold white winter passed and spring came, with patches of melting snow making the earth wet and brown.

My sister Julie, who grew prettier every year, had developed a love for music, as I had. She had a terrific singing voice and was singing with three male singers in a group called "The Sixth Day." I envied her enthusiasm.

Then one night, watching the Beverly Hillbillies, I began to think maybe I was wrong to be angry with God. Maybe he was trying to bless me and I wasn't allowing him to. During a commercial about hair spray I thought maybe I should ask his forgiveness. After the 10:00 news with Dave Moore, I went into my bedroom and got down on my knees to pray.

"Forgive me," I prayed. "I know I've been selfish and weak in faith. I've really missed out. I'm sorry, Lord. I'm really sorry."

I felt sick to my stomach, as if the ugly thoughts I had allowed to fester within me the past year were rumbling on their way up and out of me. "I'm sorry

I've blamed you for all my troubles, Lord. I want you to know that I realize my situation is not your fault. Please forgive me, Lord.

"I'm giving you my life again, all over again. Please do with me as you want. I'll try not to complain."

I prayed for a long time on my knees there on the floor. Tears slid down my cheeks. I knew the most important thing in the world was to be right with God. I needed the Christian maturity to be able to stand in the face of trials. I needed to learn how to rejoice in all things, as the Bible said. But that's not easy.

Nothing changed right away. I struggled with depression every day after that. I determined to thank him in all circumstances, however, and to trust him to do something with my life.

Then a few weeks later I heard the Al Sheehan Agency was auditioning talent for a summer job in Medora, North Dakota. I knew that the show in Medora was a family-type extravaganza held outdoors among the Badlands' rocky bluffs. Thousands of people came each year for the spectacle. I was excited about the prospect of working in the show.

When the agency called and said I had the job, I went again to my room and knelt. "Lord," I began, "I knelt here to beg your forgiveness but now I'm thanking you with my whole heart. I don't deserve your love or mercy."

I sold the van and sent a check to my friends in Rolling Meadows, then started off for North Dakota in the early hours of the morning. Driving with the others in the show across the wind-swept flat farmlands, I watched the sky become gold and arch above the flat earth. Even the earth itself turned gold. In the silence I thanked God for answering my prayers.

Chapter
Twenty-Five

I had sold my stereo and camera as well as my sound equipment in order to pay back loans. I was starting all over again.

Medora, North Dakota, was supposed to have become another Chicago, according to the dreams of Marquis de Mores, back in the time of Theodore Roosevelt's ranching days. The Marquis had great plans for a railroad station, meat packing plants, and a thriving hub of cattle industry. The Gold Seal Company restored this interesting frontier town in order to preserve an important part of American history.

The show each year in the Gold Seal Amphitheater traces the life of Theodore Roosevelt throughout and stresses our American heritage. At one point in the show a stagecoach drawn by two horses makes an entrance on the stage in an extravagant production number.

The stage of the outdoor theater is set in the side of a rock bluff not far from Theodore Roosevelt's

Maltese Cross Ranch Cabin. Some of our numbers were done from rocks. We would climb up to them on narrow wooden stairways and the spotlight would shine on us, producing an exciting spectacle.

Playing outdoors in the hot spotlights in summer presented new problems. Bugs flew into our eyes and hair and one night as I stood on one of the cliffs, singing "Maria" from *Paint Your Wagon,* I noticed a bug buzzing close to my cheek. I kept on singing, and on a high note the bug flew into my mouth. I couldn't stop the number to spit it out, so I kept on singing with it fluttering in my mouth. Then I had no alternative but to swallow it. I could feel it sliding down my throat as I sang, "—(gulp)—they call the wind Maria. . . ."

Then there was the rain. It began lightly at first but worked into a full-fledged downpour. The audience didn't leave. If the audience stays, the show stays, so we continued the entire show in the pounding rain. Our costumes, sets, animals, and props sagged and grew water-logged. I went out on the nearly flooded stage and sang, "I Believe in Music," thinking we were probably all crazy. But the people liked the show enough to stay outside, getting drenched, to see it.

Two very wonderful people named Sheila and Harold Schafer, from Bismarck, had a special interest in the show. Harold is the originator and chairman of the board of the Gold Seal Company, the makers of Snowy Bleach, Glass Wax, Mister Bubble Bubble Bath, as well as other products. The Schafers were avid fans as well as the owners of the show, and often on weekends you'd see

Harold and Sheila Schafer, my dear friends who intro-duced me to Lawrence Welk in the summer of 1973.

Harold working in the cafeteria and his wife bustling about, serving people. I was overwhelmed at their eagerness to help people and to work. They enjoyed this "ordinary" life. One day I saw Harold in the kitchen, washing dishes, while his wife took orders from customers in the cafeteria.

I never want to forget the example they set for me of love and interest in other people. I had never met such unselfish people. They actually had every opportunity to live in an ivory tower, but they loved Medora and the folks who come there. They wouldn't miss being a part of the summer's festivities.

One day I saw Sheila in the lobby of the Rough Rider Hotel. We said a friendly hello and chatted, but then our conversation turned to the Lord. We talked for three and a half hours! On Sunday morning I was asked to sing at the little church in Medora. I sang "I Asked the Lord."

Sheila told me later that as she and her husband heard me sing, they both felt they should help me with my career because they knew that what I was singing about was real in my life.

One day we met again on the street and Sheila said to me, "Tom, would you mind if we talked to Lawrence Welk about you?"

I blinked. "But what would you talk to Lawrence Welk about?"

"About giving you an audition for his show!"

I was flabbergasted, but I didn't want to get my hopes up. After all, my main purpose in being at Medora was not only to work and earn money, but to get myself close to the Lord again. The previous year had been a disaster when I had sunk into self-pity and anger at the Lord—I felt I needed the summer to read the Word, to pray, and to get to know him better.

"Lord," I prayed, "if this takes my attention away from you, I don't want it. I want it only if it is of you." And I put the idea of auditioning for Lawrence Welk out of my mind.

That is, until three weeks later when Sheila told me, "Lawrence Welk is coming to North Dakota for a family reunion! And he's coming to Bismarck to play golf. Then maybe we can take you to meet him!"

The idea sounded great, but again I was afraid to get my hopes up.

Lawrence Welk did visit his family in Strasburg and he did go to Bismarck to play golf. Sheila and Harold drove me to Bismarck with them to meet him. Now I was excited. He was playing golf at the Apple Creek Country Club with the ex-governor of the state, Bill Guy. I brought along a pianist just in case I might get a chance to sing for him.

Sheila left me in the lobby of the country club and went to find Mr. Welk, who was already on the second tee. Soon Sheila, an enormously energetic person, came running across the lobby to me. "Come on! He's on the second tee!" That could have been the planet Jupiter to me. She grabbed my hand and ran with me through the club and across the golf course and green where he was about to putt the ball into the cup. "Now don't be nervous," she whispered. "It's just Lawrence Welk." (*Just* Lawrence Welk?) Then waving and shouting, "Lawrence! Yoo-hoo, Lawrence!" she turned again to me, nudging me. "Wonderful man. You'll love him."

They embraced and chatted happily as old friends do and I stood there in my white pants and shoes and navy shirt with blue sweater (some of my outfit was borrowed), feeling very nervous indeed.

The ball slid into the cup and Lawrence turned to me and said, "Ah! Is this the young man you were telling me about?" I stepped forward on one white foot. "How do you do, sir," I said.

"He's a nice-looking young man," he said to Sheila, surveying me. "Well, do you play golf?"

"No, not well, sir."

"That's all right. Come with me and be my caddy." So I walked alongside him as he played golf, and we talked. We talked about the Lord and being a Christian in show business.

"You're right, Tom," he told me. "Christians ought to make themselves known and stand up for what's right and wrong. That's what I want on my show."

We went to the country club for lunch and I still wasn't sure whether or not I would sing for him. During our salad course he asked, "Is there any way you could manage to sing for me?"

I answered, "Well, I just happen to have brought along an accompanist. . . ."

I sang the first number. During the second number, he whispered to Sheila, "I want you to know, if I ask him to sing three songs, that means I like him."

When I finished he said, "But you had one more song to sing for me, didn't you?"

I saw Sheila beaming and rubbing her hands together. I sang, "I Asked the Lord." The people applauded, and so did the Chevrolet salesmen's convention in the next room.

Mr. Welk gave his famous smile and applauded too. He told me, "There are no openings on my television show now but I want you to come to the St. Paul Civic Center in September when we will be performing there. You can sing on the show and I'll see how that audience likes you."

I don't remember what we ate. To me it was manna from heaven.

On the 125-mile drive back to Medora I asked my accompanist, Dwight Elrich, "What do you think are my chances of actually getting on the Lawrence Welk Show?" He shook his head in a way that said, "Hopeless." He was a Christian, so I respected what he had to say.

"Tom," he said, still shaking his head, "I don't want to sound discouraging, but just look at the odds. It's a national television show. Think of all the singers in this country he has to choose from. Thousands—maybe millions. I wouldn't get my hopes up."

"You're right." I thanked the Lord for allowing me to meet Lawrence Welk and to sing for him, but I decided to put out of my mind the hope of ever appearing on his television show.

"He probably won't even remember he asked you to sing at the St. Paul Civic Center," Dwight said. "He's a busy man, after all. Think of all the people he meets each week. Tom, understand, I'm only trying to be realistic."

The summer season at Medora came to a close and I packed up my suitcase and the few extra dollars I had managed to save and headed back to Minnesota. I had no idea where I'd work next.

I didn't want to go back to real estate or selling shoes, that was for certain. Julie's boyfriend, Bruce, the leader of their singing group, asked me to sing with them. I thought I might try it. It gave me something to look forward to.

It was only a few weeks later when a couple of my friends from Bible school days were over and the telephone rang. We were down in the basement talking and laughing and listening to records when my mom appeared at the top of the stairs. She looked as though she were in a state of semi-shock. "Tom?"

"Yes, Mom?"

"Tom, you'd better come to the telephone. It's—it's Lawrence Welk!"

My friends gasped. "*Lawrence Welk?* Calling you?"

I leaped up the steps, three at a time.

"Hellooo," said one of the most familiar voices in America. "Guess who dis is!"

It really was Lawrence Welk, calling personally. "Tom," he said, "I just want to make sure you'll be at the St. Paul Civic Center when we do our show."

"Yes, sir, I'll be there!" He told me to be there a few minutes early and "just sing the songs you sang for me in North Dakota; that'll be fine." He was so gracious, you would think I was doing him a favor by consenting to show up.

Chapter
Twenty-Six

The St. Paul Civic Center is a huge hulking complex covering several blocks. I found a parking space three blocks from the main entrance and walked quickly past the little park toward the auditorium.

"Stage door?" The man in the lobby by the ticket window didn't even look up. "There ain't no stage door. Maybe you mean the loading dock. There's a loading dock. 'Round thataway." He gestured with his shoulder. "Keep following around the building."

I said thanks and walked outside. Lawrence Welk fans were pulling up in buses. Wheelchairs were lined up on the sidewalks. I nodded to a group of teen-agers who were crowded around the side of a Volkswagen van.

The doors along the building were closed and unmarked. I could hear the cars whistling past on nearby I-94 and the wind was doing terrible things with my hair.

171

I saw a ramp leading upward to a pair of broad doors. "Nope. This ain't the stage entrance, fella. You must be looking for the entrance downstairs. Just down them stairs. Around the building and then down the ramp. Can't miss it."

I wondered if Paul Newman ever went through anything like this.

The wind was blowing strong now. My hair was flying in all directions and my $15.00-plus-tip haircut now looked like the top of a pineapple. Then I saw the door from the top of the ramp behind a U-Haul truck. I approached it, wondering what or who might be behind it. Joe Namath, Harmon Killebrew, Hubert Humphrey, Morris the Cat—I stood in front of the door which didn't read "stage door" like in the movies. It said in block letters, EMPLOYEES' ENTRANCE.

Inside I found the backstage area was just a cavernous end of the auditorium. There were black curtains forming small areas designated BOYS QUICK CHANGE and GIRLS QUICK CHANGE. No props, no sets, and squinting through the darkness, I saw no people.

"Huh? You're two hours early," the man in the coveralls told me. "The Welk bus hasn't even showed up yet. You can wait around if you want to." He looked disinterested, but asked as an afterthought, "—Uh. What is it you wanted to see Mr. Welk for?"

"I'm going to sing on the show today."

"Oh." No change of expression. "Wait around then if you care to."

"Thanks." At least I had time to comb Mr. Kenneth Styles for Men back into place.

Then the cast members arrived. I watched each of them coming through the employees' entrance, and I thought of the many times their voices had filled our living room and mingled with the sounds of Brad and me wrestling and the smells of dinner on the stove. Anacani and Gail had their hair in curlers and bandanas, and wore dungarees and sneakers. The dancer, Cissy, was wearing a rumpled red jump suit, her platinum hair tucked beneath an oversized straw hat, and perched on her nose was the largest pair of spectacles I'd ever seen. (So! Stars' clothes get wrinkled, too!) I recognized most of the musicians.

The people were friendly and smiled or said Hi to me as they passed on the way to the dressing rooms. They seemed as nice as any of the people I had worked with on other shows. Maybe nicer.

Jim Roberts asked me who I was waiting for. I told him that I would be singing in the show today. He was so friendly, I felt I had known him for a long time. He called Bob Ralston over and introduced us. "Oh, yes. Lawrence told me about you. Let's go over your numbers. I'll be accompanying you."

As we quickly rehearsed my numbers, I saw the performers, one by one, come out of their dressing rooms in their makeup and costumes. I felt self-conscious, as though perhaps I had hayseed on my lapel or chicken feathers in my ears. Everybody around me seemed so Hollywood and I was feeling so—so Minnesota.

Nothing wrong with Minnesota, mind you. Some of the most beautiful people in the world are from Minnesota. My family, for instance, who were right now finding their seats in the auditorium. I knew they were excited for me, and nervous. I imagined my mom biting her lower lip and wringing her hands. Wendy would be fidgeting with her program and looking around the auditorium at the huge crowd. Brad would be there with Jennifer. And Julie would be secretly hoping I'd still want to sing with her and her group.

Harold and Sheila Schafer were there, also. They had flown in from Bismarck, rented a suite at the North Star Inn, and made arrangements for a reception following the show. They were becoming like a second mom and dad to me.

As the musicians took their places in the orchestra, I saw Lawrence Welk coming toward me. He was dressed in a powder blue suit, shirt, and shoes, and looked smaller than when I saw him in North Dakota. He was smiling a warm and friendly smile. "Are you ready to sing for the people today, Tom?"

"Yes, sir."

"That's good. Well, I'll be putting you on in the middle of the show so you just stand by and be ready. You're not nervous, are you?"

"I think I am, Mr. Welk . . . a little bit."

"I'm glad you admitted that. Shows you're honest. Well, a little nervousness never hurt a performance. It actually makes it better." Then, taking lively little steps, he hurried on stage to the thundering ovation of his fans.

Bobby and Cissy were doing their dance number when I stepped into the shadows offstage to pray. "Lord, I commit this night to you. If it is your will that it all works out, then wonderful. I'm going to have peace now that you are in control of this performance as well as my entire life. If I do well, fine. If I do terribly, then I'll know it's not your will that I get a job with Lawrence Welk."

The minutes fell away. I watched Arthur Duncan tap dance, Gail Farrell play the piano, Anacani sing, and then I heard Mr. Welk's voice near me. "Are you ready now?" He pulled some notes out of his jacket pocket and read them over. "At the end of this number by the orchestra I am going to introduce you."

I swallowed. *Dear Jesus, help me.* I felt as if I were back at Bloomington High ready to go on stage for the first time in the class play. Did Donny Osmond ever suffer like this?

Then I heard Lawrence. "Ladies and gentlemen, I have a very special surprise for you today. I want to introduce you to a young man I met in North Dakota—come on out here, Tom, and say hello to the folks." My feet moved and I was smiling and striding across the stage to the microphone. The spotlights shone on me and followed me across the gigantic stage.

"His name is Tom Netherton and he's from Bloomington, Minnesota." (Thunderous applause.) "I've asked him to come and sing for us today."

I heard Bob play my intro and I began the song, "I Asked the Lord." When the song was over, I heard an eruption of applause that stunned me. The people were shouting and applauding.

"Just listen to that applause!" Lawrence shouted. "Just listen to that audience! That was Tom Netherton, ladies and gentlemen! Tom, come over here! You better sing another song." Then nodding his head up and down to the audience he said, "Would you like that, ladies and gentlemen?"

There was an uproar of applause.

My intro began and I started, "I talk to the trees. . ."

When I finished the song the audience was clapping and shouting and waving their arms in the air. I had never heard anything like it in my life.

I bowed and started off the stage.

"You can't just leave the stage when the audience is giving you such an ovation!" Mr. Welk shouted into the microphone. His baton was stuck under his arm and he was applauding, too.

"The audience is always right, Tom," he said. Then, holding onto my sleeve, he turned to the audience and said, "Well, what do you think of him? Do you like this Minnesota boy?" The audience applauded their approval. I tried to find my family in the sea of faces.

Then Lawrence was talking to his audience as though he were talking one-to-one to old friends. "There's only one thing I can do, folks. Tom, how would you like to come out to Hollywood and be on my television show?"

My knees weakened. Hire me right *here*? On stage? In front of 19,000 people?

What did I say? Did I stutter? Did I say Yes or did I say Sure?

The crowd went absolutely wild. Right before our eyes an American dream had come true. Hometown boy makes good. That was better than a neighbor winning the lottery or some cousin running for public office. A local boy had stood up and sung a couple of tunes and as a result had an offer to go to Hollywood. How lucky can a tall, blond, all-American kid get?

And Lawrence Welk, one of the greatest showmen in the business—who knows his audiences perfectly—made it all possible.

I was overwhelmed with well-wishing people shaking my hand, patting my back, talking all at once, and asking for my autograph. As I looked into their faces I couldn't help but think of my dad, and secretly wondered how he felt about what had just happened. We hadn't always been able to understand each other, but I always knew he deeply loved me, and I hoped that today he was proud of me.

In the talk and the clamor, I sensed that somewhere in the distance, not too far, there was a dawn breaking; yellow, bright, beautiful—and the morning would follow.

Chapter
Twenty-Seven

I flew to Hollywood in October 1973, via United Airlines Flight #111. I sat in Seat J13 by the window, and my flight attendant's name was Virginia. Our in-flight meal was lasagne, and the only magazine in the complimentary reading rack was *Fortune.* I thumbed through it and put it back on the rack.

After going over the instructions on emergency procedures about fourteen times, I settled down to some serious cloud-gazing through a blank white window.

The minutes literally took hours. I left my seat for a drink of water a few times, tried to doze, cleared my throat, and prayed.

Then after what seemed like several days, maybe weeks, the captain's voice was heard over the intercom. "Ladies and gentlemen, the fasten seatbelt sign is on. We are now approaching the Los Angeles International Airport. It's a balmy day in Los Angeles today. . . ."

I tried to look out the window without pressing my nose to the glass. Beautiful, beautiful city! Down there somewhere in those gray and brown dots was the television and movie capital of the world.

The Schafers, my friends in North Dakota, had arranged to have me met at the airport and taken to Champagne Towers, Lawrence Welk's beautiful sixteen-story apartment complex in Santa Monica. It was on the corner of Ocean Avenue and Wilshire Boulevard and overlooked the Pacific Ocean. Adjoining was a twenty-one-story office building, forming Lawrence Welk Plaza.

Once inside the exquisite guest apartment, I stood holding my breath as I surveyed my elegant surroundings. Then I found a telephone (in a decorator casing) and dialed the Lawrence Welk production office to tell them I had arrived. I learned I was to be at the offices the next day to sing for the television production staff.

A performer would appear on the show once as a kind of screen test/audition. The production staff could then observe how the performer looks in front of the camera and the audience response he receives. There would be another consultation later to decide whether or not the performer would remain on the show as a permanent member of the cast. There are no contracts. Lawrence doesn't need them. Most of the people who work for him stay with him. He has a great record for keeping performers and musicians.

I walked around the apartment, looking out of the large windows to the ocean below as it thumped against the beach. I sat in all the chairs. I pushed all the buttons. (There were buttons for the drapes, which opened and closed electronically.) Everything was color-coordinated. The master bedroom was in various shades of gold. I stretched across the gold, king-sized bed and called home.

"It's I, Thomas H. Netherton, Jr.," I sang, "calling from the great Pacific Ocean where I am completely surrounded in gold."

"Oh, so it all panned out, eh, Tom?" Brad joked back at me.

At 7:45 the next morning, I was still asleep between the gold-colored sheets when the telephone in the gold casing by the bed rang. I lifted the receiver.

"Hellooo," sang the unmistakable voice of Lawrence Welk. "Guess who dis is!" I answered correctly. He commented that I was a late riser and then chatted happily about how I guessed right away who it was and to be sure to be there by ten o'clock because they would all be so anxious to see me.

Before he hung up he said, "By the way, there's a strike on at the television studios. If it doesn't end, we won't be having a show for a while, but you come over to the office anyway and sing for us."

When I arrived, Mr. Welk introduced me to Jack Imel, the assistant producer, George Cates, the conductor, Jim Hobson, the producer, arrangers Curt Ramsey and Joe Rizzo and Myron Floren.

I sang "If Ever I Would Leave You." They conferred, then had me sing another song. When I finished, they seemed pleased. Then Lawrence began talking about my voice. George had me try doing something different, stressing the vibrato on the full note instead of only at the end of a note. I did as directed and Lawrence beamed.

"Well! What do you think?" he exclaimed. "Doesn't he learn quickly? Don't you think we should put him on the show?"

My heart stopped beating.

"But Lawrence, we always do an on-camera audition first. Don't you think we should just try him out first?"

"The audience will take to him, I'm sure of it," Lawrence said, smiling at me. "I think he should go home and get his things. I think he should move to Hollywood and join our musical family."

The short quick jabs going on in my chest couldn't be a heartbeat.

The others said, "You're usually right, Lawrence. Tom, looks like you've got a job."

My mind told my mouth to say something, something clever.

"I, uh . . . thank you—" I stammered.

Chapter
Twenty-Eight

Back in Minnesota my family was so excited, you would have thought I had just been elected governor of the state. I packed my things and prepared to go back to California. Mom fussed over me, refolding what I had folded, pressing what didn't need pressing, and taping boxes that were already taped from top to bottom.

"Oh, Tom," she said, sniffling as she repolished a pair of my shoes, "I'll never forget when you were just a little boy. . . ."

"Mom, I'm not taking those shoes."

"And you had just gotten your first two-wheeler . . ."

"Those shoes are too old. They're out of style."

"Just think of it . . . It was only yesterday."

"Mom, where is my letter opener? The white one with all the sea shells Grandpa brought me from Florida?"

"To think that you were once that little boy who

had to climb onto a box to get up on your two-wheeler."

"I can't find the letter opener."

"You were so . . . determined." She wiped away a tear.

"Mom, you know the letter opener Grandpa brought back when they took that trip to Florida?"

"And then the box tipped over right on top of you and the bike went crashing to the ground."

"I'll just have to find it myself."

"But you didn't cry. Oh, no, not Tom. You just got right back up on that box and tried all over again."

"Mom, for heaven's sake!"

"Don't you remember, Tom? You were so cute."

I sat down beside her on the bed. "Mom, it's you who are cute. And you are also beautiful. And I love you."

"Tom, I'm just so—proud of you."

"And you're the best mother in the whole world. I have something to ask you, however—"

"It's in the dresser where you left it, silly."

"Thanks!"

"And listen, Tom, you shouldn't really take those shoes—they're out of style."

I arrived in Hollywood while the strike at the television studio was still going strong. Back in Minnesota I hadn't felt I ought to continue to stay at Champagne Towers at Lawrence Welk's expense when I wasn't working for him yet, so I had called Erna Moorman, the soprano I had worked with in the Medora show. She and her husband and family were Christians who lived in Santa Monica. They were happy to hear my voice over the telephone.

"Of course you'll stay with us! We'd love to have you!"

They gave me their little boy's room, so I slept in a short child's bed with pictures of baseball heroes all around me. I actually began to enjoy waking up to teddy bears, baseball gloves, and photos of the Dodgers.

Erna was a busy singer and did many recording dates. She took me with her to one of her recording sessions, where she was doing a song on a John W. Petersen recording. I met people at the studio I had watched on television or heard about for years. For example, Thurl Ravenscroft, a singer with the Johnny Mann singers who also does the voice of Tony the Tiger. I also met Mr. Petersen, who was working on a new musical, and another Christian arranger and musician whose work I admired, a young composer named Paul Johnson.

I heard Paul's music and thought he was a genius at writing beautiful melodies and deep lyrics. I told him so. He was obviously happy that I admired his work so much. He was friendly and kind and invited me to his church. A few weeks later I saw him again and he asked me if I had found a permanent place to live yet. I told him No, and he invited me to come and look at his place to see if I'd like to move in there, because his room-mate had just gotten married.

It was a gorgeous bachelor-pad in Woodland Hills, with thick brown carpeting, beamed ceilings, elaborate stereo equipment and a grand piano. It was a musician's paradise. I moved in the next day. By now the strike at the television studios was over and rehearsal was called for my first telecast.

Erna's husband loaned me his car to get to the studio, so I went to my first rehearsal in real class. I pulled into the ABC parking lot in a shining silver 240Z Datsun sports car. Mary Lou Metzger and Sandi Griffith, two of the girls on the show, saw me drive past. Later they joked, "Looks like you're doing pretty well without this show, Tom!" I had to confess the car wasn't mine. Quietly to myself I thought, "Someday I will have one of my own."

Studio E was a huge cave-like hall with high ceilings dripping hundreds of heavy lights on cables. The lights caught my attention first and then the stage itself, with the orchestra already set up and lit. The musicians were in place, and George Cates, with his baton poised, stood before them. A voice called over the loudspeaker, "All right, George, Number Two, Number Two."

The sound of the full orchestra filled the studio as well as the halls outside. Cissy and Bobby practiced a time-step at the side of the stage. Anacani, Tanya, and Ralna were standing offstage, waiting and listening to the orchestra tune up.

"All right," the voice on the loudspeaker said. It was Jim Hobson, our producer. "Stand by for the opening." There was a scramble as Ken, Art, Joe, and Guy moved to their places on stage. "We're going to do the opening number without the fanfare. Just the opening number. Stand by."

There were cameramen, stage hands, and lighting people everywhere. I asked one of the cameramen, who was wearing a tee shirt with THE

BOBBY GOLDSBORO SHOW written across it,
"How many people work on this show?"

He answered, laughing, "About half of them."

A small blonde lady stood by my side, listening to
the directions coming over the loudspeaker. I
looked down and recognized her at once as Norma
Zimmer.

"Hi," she said cheerfully. I introduced myself and
she seemed genuinely delighted that I was going to
be on the show. "Oh, I'm so *happy* you're going to
be with us, Tom. God bless you!" Norma would
become a dear friend, one who would be a constant
source of quiet inspiration. I was to learn soon why
millions of people love her.

Then I met the others, one by one. They seemed
so small! Particularly the girls, who on television
looked much taller than they actually were in person. I had no idea they were so petite. But then, for
me, any girl who was under six feet was short.

Soon I was in a hubbub of activity. The people
were crowded around me and I was introduced to
what seemed like dozens of people working on the
show. Each one gave me a warm and friendly welcome.

The voice on the loudspeaker was heard again.

"OK, stand by, please. Bobby, can you move
stage right? Norma, back up a little bit just for the
opening shot . . . Can that light tree go back any?
OK, stand by—Sandi, you're right in front of the
camera. OK. Cue it."

The orchestra swelled, then died.

"Jack, wait four bars. Go back to position, kids.
If you don't have time, we'll give you the whole sixteen—Stand by, please. Cue it, George."

I stood watching the performers go through their paces, singing full voice, even though it was early in the morning. This was the first rehearsal of the day, then in the afternoon there would be another. At 5:15 we would do the dress rehearsal before a studio audience. At 8:00 we did the taping.

Jack Imel, the assistant producer, took me across the stage to meet the costumer, Rose Weiss. Rose, an attractive woman wearing a blue suit and lots of jewelry, took one look at me, threw her hands in the air, and screamed. She looked me up and down from head to toe, moaning, "If you think I can costume him in the clothes the other kids wear, you're crazy!" I would be a problem to her because most of the other guys wore average sizes. I didn't.

Jack showed me my dressing room upstairs over the studio and I sat down to sigh a prayer of thanks. I wanted to hold on to the moment because it was one of the happiest in my life.

"Stand by, please, on Number Three."

Then I heard the voices of Guy and Ralna and I knew it would soon be my turn.

Rose had a size 44 Extra Long jacket for me to wear and I stood for a fitting with the guys in wardrobe pinning it from behind.

"Just don't turn around, Tom," they told me. "Keep facing the cameras." I couldn't move very well, but from the front I looked pretty good.

"I don't know what they think I am," Rose complained. "They expect me to be a magician, maybe?" I recognized warmth and humor beneath her grumblings.

I smiled. "Oh, Rose, you'll grow to love me, you wait."

"Just as long as *you* don't do any more growing, kiddo! And I thought Hoopie had long arms!"

The excitement of the studio was everywhere. That excitement carried over to the commissary, where I saw people from other shows having lunch. People from the "Sonny Bono Show," "Let's Make a Deal," and "General Hospital." The man in front of me in line at the cash register with a bottle of mixed fruit juice was Monty Hall.

The greatest thrill that first day, however, was when the cameras poised in front of me and I began my number. I thought, 35 million people behind that camera—35 million people across the country were going to be watching me. I took a breath, smiled, and sang, "Take my hand, I'm a stranger in paradise . . ."

The next week we rehearsed and taped the Christmas special and this was actually the first show of mine that was aired. Lawrence was so gracious and generous to me on that show. I sang "Silent Night" and he played it on the organ for me. Later he said, "What did I tell you? The audience loves you!" Having Lawrence support me like that on camera made a big difference in the audience's acceptance of me.

We had prayer meetings at Paul's house with other Christians in show business. We talked about pride and jealousy and the things that can be a problem to people in our work. We shared our hopes and dreams and prayed for one another. Each of us shared the conviction that the Lord had placed us where we were and we wanted to glorify him in all we did.

I loved these prayer meetings. I felt at last that I belonged and wasn't an outsider any longer. During my years in show business, I was usually the one person in church who wasn't like everyone else, because I was a performer. There are usually two opinions about my profession. One: It is sinful and I should get out before it's too late, or two: It's a life for a worldly Christian. That hurt because a worldly Christian is one who does not acknowledge the Lordship of Jesus—and Jesus *was* Lord in my life.

At our prayer meetings we were able to talk about these things because they are things which cause confusion and pain. We were able to pray together, read and study the Word, and worship God together. These people, I found, were dedicated Christians whose testimonies touched literally millions of people all over the world.

Chapter
Twenty-Nine

After a few months on the show, I began receiving fan letters. I was overwhelmed that so many people would want to write to me. Most of the mail came from young people who wrote the kind of letter you'd write to a good friend. They would tell me things like: "My sister Susan is getting married next month on the sixteenth, and I'll be able to go home for three days. It's a fourteen-hour drive." Or, "Our Little League baseball team is playing again tonight. We're very proud of our Peter and his 300th hit." Or, "Dad is coming home late from work tonight so we are going to have a late supper. Boy, it's cold outside. The wind is estimated at fifty-one miles per hour."

Then there were the letters that asked, "How can I know the Lord the way you know him?" and "Is God really real?"

Responding to fan mail began taking up more and more of my time, and soon my answers were being sent out months late. I simply couldn't keep up. I needed help and I needed it fast. Then a brilliant idea flashed into my mind. I knew a lady who would be perfect as a part-time secretary if only she would do it. She was a warm, intelligent, sensitive Christian, and extremely efficient. She was a wonderful friend and I loved her very much. She was also my father's mom, Ruth Netherton, whom the family all affectionately called "Gramma."

I called her and told her about my idea, and was overjoyed when she said she would help. I went to see her at her apartment and when she opened the door, I gave her a big hug and kiss. I thought to myself how wonderfully she takes care of herself—smooth delicate complexion, her gray hair attractively styled. She was beautifully groomed and had a loving twinkle in her eye. I knew that same love and care would be put into helping me answer my fan mail.

There was talk about recording an album, and Paul Johnson, who had written many beautiful songs, contacted Word Records about me. But at the time they weren't very enthusiastic, so Paul's dad put up the money, and late in 1974 we recorded my first album, *What a Friend*, on our own. I couldn't believe that Dr. Johnson could have such faith in Paul and me. But it paid off, because Word bought the rights to the album, and I've been a Word artist ever since.

The song, "Lord, Take Control of Me," which Paul wrote, was a particular favorite of mine. I included a beautiful number on the album, "Mother, I Love You," because I thought it was one thing to call home and say "I love you, Mom," and another thing to sing it to her on an album. She was over-whelmed when she heard it. She wept and called her friends and told them stories about when I was a child.

I called her up and began to laugh when I heard her sniffles over the telephone. "Listen, Mom, have you told everyone about my little gray runaway car?"

"Oh, I'd forgotten about that!"

Then she instructed me to take my vitamins, double up on the C's, it's getting colder and good-bye, this is costing you a fortune.

We went on tour that year and I had my first taste of one-night stands. In ten days we played Rapid City, Ames, St. Paul, South Bend, Huntington, Pittsburgh, Niagara Falls, Springfield, Binghamton and Champaign. Later in the summer we played a three-week engagement at Harrah's in Lake Tahoe.

The stay at beautiful Lake Tahoe was more like a vacation. The people in the show brought their families and we relaxed and enjoyed the magnificent pine-covered mountains and icy lake.

Anacani, the pretty Mexican singer on the show, and I became good friends. We often drove together on the two-hour trek to Escondido to sing at Lawrence's restaurant there. Anacani was a kind and down-to-earth girl. We had some super talks and she asked questions about the Lord. The fan magazine *Movieland* did a photo story of us, and so did *Photo Screen*. Since we were dating, both articles talked about our "romance," and they also included my Christian testimony.

One day at the television studio in Los Angeles,

Lawrence called me into his dressing room. "Tom, how would you like to play a date on your own? You'd be the headliner for a Northwest Airline convention."

"Headliner? Mr. Welk, you're kidding."

"They're willing to pay $1,200. Will that be enough?"

I was flabbergasted. $1,200! "Certainly!"

I thought about the concerts I had performed for an average pay of $25.00 per concert, including travel expenses. "When do I have to start rehearsing?"

I began to work with a talented arranger I knew, putting together an act for that event, but I had no idea of what lay ahead for me when, in another couple of years, I'd have to put together a major night club act. Then it would involve many more people than just two of us. By then I would have a manager, a producer-choreographer, a musical director, many arrangers, and the cost would be ten times the amount I was spending now.

Preparing for my first act now, I was basically on my own, but for the night club act I would have the assistance of some of the best people in Hollywood. (Joe Parnello would be my musical director. He worked with Vic Damone for years, as well as with Bobby Vinton. Hugh Lambert, Nancy Sinatra's husband, would do the choreography, and Nelson Riddle, Don Costa, and Joe Parnello would do the arrangements.)

Now I was working day and night, going over music, selecting arrangements, and putting together my first solo act.

The response to the show for Northwest Airlines

was overwhelming. They even gave me a standing ovation.

Soon the Wayne Coombs Agency was booking me regularly for Christian concerts in churches, and I was appearing on television programs like "The 700 Club," "High Adventure," and the "PTL Club."

I moved to my own apartment in Toluca Lake and one of the purchases I made was a 280Z Datsun sports car. I remembered driving into the ABC lot over two years before in a borrowed 240Z and thinking how nice it would be to own my own sports car. I thought of my exchange student friend in Peru with his XKE. I felt on top of the world.

My calendar began to fill up with secular singing dates across the country because of the efforts of Dick Shack at the Agency for Performing Arts. They would eventually have me headlining at the Royal York Hotel in Toronto, the Fairmont Hotel in New Orleans, as well as fairs and conventions across the country.

Performing at the fairs was exciting and fun. The fans always made it interesting. Once, at a performance in Massachusetts, I was about to go on stage when suddenly from out of nowhere a woman weighing at least 250 pounds leaped at me. She grabbed me in a hammerlock around the throat. "I love you! You're my favorite!" she shouted. I was startled and almost lost my balance. "I'll never let you go!" she yelled. "Never! I'll never let you go! You're my favorite!"

I heard my intro and gasped, "Lady, I have to be

on stage!" Her hold tightened. "I'll never let you go!"

I took a breath, grabbed her hands and sprung them apart, causing my release, like a pea out of a pod. She was stunned. "But you're my favorite!" she yelled. She stood there like a defeated lady wrestler and I just barely got on stage for my music cue. I was a bit breathless and thought it humorous when I sang, "You are too beautiful for one man alone. . . ."

I especially loved performing my Christian concerts. One night, after I had just finished doing a concert in a large midwestern church, I got to talking with a group of the young Christians. A handsome young man told me, "You know, sometimes I feel like my testimony is so dull. I've never been on drugs, never been in jail, never been an alcoholic . . . in fact, I've gone to church most of my life and can't even remember a time when I didn't love the Lord."

I listened.

"The testimonies we hear in church and the stories we hear are never about people like me. I feel so—so *ordinary.*"

The others in the group nodded their heads in agreement.

"Oh, but nobody who loves the Lord is ordinary!" I exclaimed. "The people who have suffered because of drugs, alcohol, or reckless living are precious and very important to the Lord, but so are the ones who have never known these things."

I am one of the most ordinary people in the world. I hope I never think of myself as anything more than ordinary. Sometimes people look at me and think I've got one of the easiest lives there could be. But I believe that life is what you make it to be.

I told the young man about a girl I met who went to pieces when she broke a fingernail. It was practically the end of the world to her. Then there are the people who have suffered through wars, poverty, and persecution, and have risen up smiling and mighty in the Lord.

The Christian life is what we make it to be. Being a Christian ought to be exciting, in fact, it should be the most exciting life in the world.

"My testimony is my life *now*," I said as the group gathered around me. "And so is yours. I've never been on drugs, either. And I've never been an alcoholic. But I know what it is to live without Christ. Life for ordinary people like you and me is the greatest life there is."

A pretty young girl in glasses and a floor-length dress with ruffled sleeves said, "People call me a goodie-goodie because I don't go to wild parties and I don't swear or tell off-color stories. Even my parents think I'm weird."

"And Jesus calls you Beloved and he thinks you're beautiful. Who are you going to listen to and believe?"

As we talked, I silently prayed that these young people would realize how valuable and lovely they were in the eyes of God.

For as long as I could remember I wanted my life to count for something. When I had discovered my life actually *did* count and that I was an important person, it was not because of my accomplishments or my good life, or even because I had come through suffering and could talk about it. My life counted because it belonged to the Lord Jesus, every moment of it and every part of it. This is what made me important, and this is what gave me my true identity.

The young man shook my hand and asked me to pray for him. All of us bowed our heads and prayed together right there on the stage of the auditorium with crowds of people around us. I felt at once a part of these young people, one of them. I understood their aches and their longings; I knew what it was like to be ordinary and to be, like the girl said, "a goodie-goodie." As we prayed, I felt the presence of the Lord with each one of us. We were more than a small knot of young people on a church platform. We were young people everywhere. We were the drug addicts and the pushers, the teen-age prostitutes, the hippies, the down-and-outers, the up-and-outers, and we were also the lonely church kids looking for a place in this world. We were the achievers and the nonachievers, the fatherless, the lost. We were the pastors' children, the missionary kids, the new convert kicking amphetamines and tobacco. We were large and small, we were his and all that we had to bring to him, we brought. We prayed together, "Here we are, Lord, take us just as we are. We are yours." In the beauty of the moment and our oneness with all believers everywhere, we knew he did and always would.

I left that night for Los Angeles, back to the warm air of California, where industry and business empires crowd the city, but where stucco houses with painted roofs, shutters, and awnings also line the streets. I picked up my car at the airport parking lot and drove past golden-tassled acacia, eucalyptus, and palm trees and finally arrived at my apartment. I went out on my balcony, where I sat gazing at the Verdugo Mountains, purple in the distance. I sat there until the morning crept across the sky, sat there watching, watching, as the morning arrived and enveloped me with its arms. I wanted to pray but I couldn't. I just sat there, listening to the morning sounds and watching.

Finally I got up, went inside to my bedroom, and fell into a weary sleep. I wanted to talk to someone, share the beautiful experiences I had known at the various concerts, but there was nobody I knew who would be up at that hour.

I was beginning to experience something that I didn't think would ever rear its head in my life again. It gnawed at me, slowly, quietly, painfully. It was loneliness.

Chapter Thirty

We rehearsed and did three more telecasts, and then I flew to Florida to appear in another concert. This time it was to be in a large church of over 3,000 members.

When I arrived at the church I saw there were policemen directing traffic and cars lined up for what seemed like miles. My mouth dropped open. "Where are all these people going?" I asked the taxi driver.

"They're going to hear Tom Netherton," said the driver. "He's doing a concert here tonight. Quite a turnout, eh?"

In a small room in the church I dressed for the performance and then stood off the sanctuary watching as the church filled with people. I began to pray for the people, as I always did before a performance, but I felt empty and alone.

Just then a woman approached me. "Tom—you *are* Tom Netherton?"

"Yes, I am. Hi."

"Well, excuse me, but I wonder if I could talk to you for a moment."

"Oh! Certainly."

"I am a housewife and I have six children," she said. "I've tried to raise them as best I could. They go to church, this church in fact, and they're basically wonderful kids."

"That's nice to hear," I said, smiling, and watching the people crowding in the aisles.

"The thing is that at school the rest of the kids have these rock idols and movie idols they go crazy over—people who lead miserable lives and who suggest to the kids that their lives are glamorous and exciting. What I mean is, these people are the trend-setters for the kids today. The kids imitate their life style. Look at Janis Joplin, Jimi Hendrix—look at the lives they led and the horrible deaths they died. Look at Judy Garland, Sal Mineo; even Freddie Prinze who died so tragically."

"Yes, I know," I said, and looked at her face with its fine lines. Her words were slow and deliberate.

"Tom, there aren't many heroes for the kids to look up to, do you know what I mean? Not many heroes that point the kids in the right direction."

She had my full attention.

"You just don't see many shows on television that inspire faith or that convey the idea that good clean living is OK. Almost everything you see nowadays promotes sex, violence."

"I think I know what you're saying."

"That's why I wanted to tell you personally, Tom, how much you mean to me as a parent. My children watch you every week on television. They're here tonight to hear the concert. See, you represent to them someone who makes the Christian life look good!"

I was deeply moved.

"I'm thankful for you, believe me," she said. "I'm thankful that your testimony is strong and that every week you appear on that screen, wholesome and clean-cut, showing to us and our children that being wholesome and clean-cut is good and not, if you'll pardon the expression, square. Thank you."

She smiled, patted my arm, turned, and was gone.

I fought tears throughout the entire performance. I felt enormous love for that audience. In fact, I felt something I felt in most of my performances, that the people in the audiences were my friends, people I liked and who liked me in return. I had begun to feel my best friends were my audiences, strangers actually, and that the me who sat alone in airplanes and taxis was not the real me at all.

I wished I could say it was always worth all the loneliness.

The next day I flew to Birmingham, Alabama, for a concert at Rock Methodist Church, and then to Toronto, Fort Myers, Sarasota, Florida, and then to Wichita Falls, Texas.

When I returned to Los Angeles, we began preparations for the Lawrence Welk tour. In ten days we would play El Paso; New Orleans; Birmingham; Columbia; Savannah; Lakeland, Florida; St. Petersburg; Miami; Mobile; and Shreveport; then back to Los Angeles for one day before I left alone for Winfield, Alabama, and Sioux Falls, South Dakota, for two more concerts.

My life of traveling, concerts, rehearsals, and telecasts didn't give me much time for close friendships. I would find myself coming home dragging my feet and feeling sorry for myself.

Sometimes I'd call my family in Minnesota or I'd call a girl friend I was dating. But friendships were on the telephone or they were an evening here, a dinner there.

I prayed for a wife, and then with every girl I met, I wondered if she was Miss Right. I grew exhausted looking. I lost my sense of humor over everything. The most hilarious thing in the world could happen and I'd just grunt and feel sorry for myself because I didn't find it funny.

I was in bad shape.

One night I was having dinner with a beautiful young actress who was on the brink of a big break in her career. She was not a Christian and it was not hard to tell by the way she talked. For over an hour she discussed herself and her career. I listened and didn't say much. Actually, she did most of the talking so I couldn't say much. She said, "Tom, I will do *anything* to be a star. Anything."

"That's the most depressing thing I've heard in a long time," I said.

"What do you mean, depressing? It's a *fact*. I am going to be a very big star. I am going to make it *big*, you wait and see."

I took a swallow of my coffee. "I feel sorry for you," I said.

She looked insulted.

"I mean that," I said. "Being a star has nothing to do with being a person."

"Well, you should talk. You're on your way to being a star, aren't you?"

I could have told her that what I wanted most was someone to know me and really find me a terrific *person*. But I didn't.

"I think your goals are empty and meaningless," I said.

"Listen, you may think what you want, but I'm going to be a huge star and I don't care how I do it or who I step on to get there."

"Hey! This is getting worse."

"I mean it, Tom. You just watch me."

"One thing I'll say," I said, picking up the check, "I know with all my heart and soul you don't have to step on or hurt anyone to be successful."

We left the restaurant and I told her simply, "The difference between you and me is that I want God to be in charge of my career and you don't. I hope someday you'll realize that your life will never be a real success without him."

She looked as though I had condemned her, but I hadn't. I felt sorry for her.

That night I looked over the plans for the new house I was having built and I realized how blessed I was. I realized how much anguish the Lord spared me. My life was void of striving for success, of plotting my route to fame and fortune. I realized that even though I had allowed myself a case of maximum self-pity, he was still with me, watching over me, guiding me and loving me.

I did ask him to forgive me that night. I was recording a new album, *Just As I Am*, and I told him, "Lord, just as the song says, I give myself to you just as I am. I give you a lonely man who needs you more than ever."

I reminded myself Jesus is the best friend we will ever have. He is the faithful friend, the always-loving friend and protector. When I have a business negotiation, a contract, a financial decision to make, I need to know that the Lord is watching over my business matters, that he is the one who is in full control. I have managers, attorneys, agents, advisors, and others I work alongside, but it's the Lord who is my Number One Manager. He is the custodian of all my affairs.

When I realize this, and allow myself plenty of time to read the Word and to pray, I know that it's not Tom Netherton I need to spend my time thinking about, but how Tom Netherton can best serve the Lord.

I had a dream once, a dream that was to have a powerful effect on my life. I was on tour in the Northwest and I fell asleep after an exhausting day. I dreamed I was walking through a very old and run-down section of some town. The houses were shabby, unkempt, and the people on the street looked at me through hollow, tortured eyes. Then I saw an open wooden doorway, and in the darkness there was a small, unmoving form. I walked over to it and saw that it was a person lying propped up against the door, more dead than alive. I peered at the face and saw it was an old woman, her face sunken and deeply lined. I backed away in horror.

But I couldn't leave her there like that. I turned around and went back to her and picked her up in my arms. She was so light, she barely weighed anything. I folded her in a white sheet and then I walked through the streets with her in my arms.

She was pathetic, unloved, lost, and half-starved. Tears streaked down my face as I carried her along the street. Then I found a hospital and I carried her down the long white corridor to a room where a doctor waited. She looked up at me and must have realized someone was helping her. A faint smile came to her lips and she began to cry.

When I put her on a bed, she looked up at me and smiled such a sweet pitiful smile that I felt my heart break. Then she saw the doctor and knew that everything was going to be OK.

Someone cared enough to help her.

I awoke at 4:00 A.M. to find my face wet with tears. I turned on the light by the bed and sat their continuing to weep. It was such a vivid dream that I couldn't get the woman's face out of my mind.

"Lord," I prayed, "help me be the kind of man who can help people in real life as well as in a dream." I remembered the Indians in Peru, sickly and impoverished, and I thought of my own self-centered existence.

So much of my own loneliness has been caused by selfishness. I've been too involved with me and not involved enough with Jesus. I hoped he would remind me when I felt lonely that others were lonely, too, and needed help.

Chapter
Thirty-One

At rehearsal I received the music for my number on the next telecast. I read it and decided I couldn't sing it.

"But what's the matter with the song?"

"Well, it says to say a little prayer and no matter what you believe, you'll get relief."

"Well, what's wrong with that?"

"I don't believe that. I can't sing it."

"Now, I've heard everything. Why can't you sing it? It's a nice song."

"I can't sing those lyrics:

> No matter what your belief,
> A prayer sent now and then to God
> Will bring great relief.

"So now what do we do? He won't sing the song."

"Call the songwriter. Ask him to change the words," I said.

"He'll never do it."

"So try it. What can you lose?"

I waited, rereading the words and reconfirming that I couldn't sing the song as it was written.

"OK. It's OK. You can change the words."

"May I sing 'be strong in your belief' instead of 'no matter what your belief'?"

"Sure. He says it's fine. Go ahead. Whatever."

"Thank you."

There are a lot of inspirational songs with trite lyrics that say nothing. A prayer to "anything" said now and then couldn't possibly bring much relief. Who are we praying to? A flower? A tree? "Hello, tree, it's me, Tom. Please bring me relief." Ridiculous.

I began to notice that trumpeter Johnny Zell was usually morose and off by himself. He was an enormously talented musician and yet he was such a sad person. We often sat together on the airplanes on tour and would talk about the Lord. He listened and asked questions and then went on his sad way.

We ate together in the commissary one day and he questioned me again. "How do you know that Jesus Christ is really the Savior? I mean, how do you know for *sure*?"

"Why don't you ask him to answer that for you, Johnny?"

"Huh?"

"Why don't you ask him to prove to you who he is? Just ask him."

Johnny didn't say anything for the rest of the meal. Then he went off by himself again and I didn't see much of him until a couple of days later.

Top left: **My first appearance on the Lawrence Welk Show, Christmas 1973. Lawrence accompanied me as I sang "Silent Night."** *Top right:* **Bob Smale, pianist; Tom Netherton, soloist.** *Bottom left:* **I couldn't resist giving a kiss to this sweet lady guard in Maumee, Ohio.** *Bottom right:* **One thing about my job—I get to sing to a lot of pretty girls!**

He came to my dressing room and stood in the doorway. "Hi!" I said. "Come on in." He sat on one of the comfortable chairs along the wall.

"Well, Tom, I think I understand what you've been talking about all this time."

"You do?"

"Yes. I asked the Lord Jesus to prove himself to me and I gave my life to him. I'm a Christian, too."

"Johnny!"

"I just want to thank you, Tom. I think you are a big talent, but I think you're even a greater *person*—I mean that. I'll always be grateful to you, man."

Beautiful, the way the Lord answers prayer!

The people on the Lawrence Welk show are unusually friendly and as warm in real life as they are on the television screen. The new members, like Kathy Sullivan, the Otwell twins, and the Aldrich sisters are no exception.

Often on a show like ours where there are more than fifty people involved and the rehearsals are long and tedious, there isn't time to get to know each other very well. But we honestly enjoy one another and I've rarely seen any serious fights or disagreements among the cast members.

Ava Barber joined Lawrence about the same time I did. In fact, she auditioned at Champagne Towers that day in September right after I did. She has a great sense of humor and I love to tease her. She screams with laughter when I tell her that one day when she is a hugely famous superstar I'm going to buy a bus and get rich, driving tourists by her house. I'll say, "And this is the home of the famous

Ava Barber, folks! I used to know her Way Back When. . . ." Then I pantomime calling up to her in her palatial nest with a megaphone: "Yoo-hoo! Ava! Down here! It's me, Tom! . . . What do you mean, 'Tom who?' Well, folks, you saw it first on Netherton Tours." Ava rocks with laughter and in her Knoxville accent says, "Tom, you are ca-razy!"

Since that first day when I started on the show, my costumes and suits were being basted and pinned from the back. "Smile pretty, honey, and don't turn around," they'd tell me, hoping I'd hold together long enough to finish my number.

One night after I had finished singing and the audience was still applauding, Lawrence came over to me and put his arm around me.

"Ladies and gentlemen," he said into the camera, "performers have little tricks that you don't know about. Tom, why don't you turn around and show the people some of the tricks of our trade?"

He couldn't be serious!

He grinned and turned me around so that not only the studio audience, but the 35 million viewers across America, saw the back of me stitched and pinned together like a rag doll.

The audience screamed with laughter and I shrank about four inches.

Rose was horrified. She is proud of her costuming, as well she ought to be. She makes us look terrific every week. I was a hard one to fit, but from that night on, all my clothes have been stitched from the inside.

Some of the zaniest times we have are when we are on tour. On one tour we were playing St.

Top: *Having dinner with Ralna and Guy and Mary Lou and Richard at Harrah's in 1977.* Center: *A country setting! (l. to r.): Guy and Ralna, Bobby and Cissy, me, Sandi Griffith, Ken Delo, Anacani, Joe Feeney, Gail Farrell, Norma Zimmer, and Jimmy Roberts.* Bottom: *Surrounded by pretty girls: Mary Lou, Anacani, Tanya, Gail, Sandi, and Cissy.*

Petersburg, Florida, where we had an afternoon show as well as an evening show. We had a couple of hours between shows, so Bobby Burgess, Ken Delo, and I decided to go out to get something to eat. We knew of a place called Aunt Hattie's where the food is terrific, so we changed clothes, went out the stage door, and were crossing the parking lot when suddenly I heard, "Look! There's the new boy!"

"And there's Ken Delo!"

"And that looks like Bobby Burgess!"

We stopped and looked behind us and saw what appeared to be a stampede coming at us. I was stunned, and stood paralyzed in my tracks, but Ken and Bobby, who were more experienced, said, "Run!"

Bobby ran in one direction, Ken in another, and I took off in still another direction. Then I saw a new crowd of people rushing toward me screaming, "It's Tom Netherton!" and I turned to run another direction. I felt like Gene Autry escaping the bandits. (I was happy for my track years back in high school.) I caught up with Ken, who was hopping over cars and ducking behind posts. "What's happening?" I yelled. He was laughing so hard at me, he had difficulty keeping his pace. Just then another crowd of people saw us and charged. I thought we could get killed. "Isn't it wonderful to be so *loved*?" Ken shouted.

We escaped and made it to the restaurant in time to meet Bobby who was running top speed down the street toward us. "They tried to tear my clothes off!" he panted.

Lawrence is laughing because he just turned me around so the audience could see the pins in the back of my jacket.

When we walked into the restaurant, we found it packed with Lawrence Welk fans who had just seen the show. The place erupted in applause when we were spotted at the door. There we stood, disheveled and gasping for breath in a sea of clapping and hurrahs.

One lady who came to our table for an autograph said, "My goodness, you people don't look anything like I thought you would. Why, you're all *sweating*."

The Ken Doll image of me was destroyed.

Some people are too shy to come up and ask for an autograph, however. When we returned from tour that year I had a concert in Lincoln, Illinois, and was sitting on the airplane en route there. I was relaxing and just ready to close my eyes to take a nap when I saw a hand poke through the crack between the seats. In the hand was a piece of paper. I reached down and took the piece of paper and opened it. It read, "Dear Mr. Netherton: Could I please have your autograph? Thank you very much."

I smiled to myself and wrote on the paper, "God bless you, Tom Netherton," placed the note back into the hand and watched it slip back through the crack in the seat. I never saw the person who belonged to the hand.

When I got to the airport, a woman recognized me and ran up to me breathlessly and asked in a flustered voice, "Oh, Tom Netherton! May I please have my autograph?"

When I signed my name on the paper she had given me, she sighed nervously and said, "Oh, Tom, I'm one of my greatest fans!"

My sister Julie and her husband Bruce.

My sister Julie was getting married and I promised her I'd fly home and sing at the wedding. When I sang "Sunrise, Sunset," I felt somewhat choked up. She looked so pretty in her wedding gown as I sang, "Is this the little girl I carried. . . ." Her new husband, Bruce, was a talented musician and songwriter, and I was happy Julie had found someone who would really appreciate her for the special person she was.

My records had begun selling well, which pleased me. In 1974 I recorded *My Favorite Hymns* on the Ranwood Label. I received many letters from people who told me how much they enjoyed the album. One lady wrote that she played it every Sunday morning. She said it was her way of going to church. I wrote back that I was delighted she enjoyed the record, but that it would be good for her to attend a church, as well.

One day I received a very sweet letter from a seventy-year-old woman who was concerned about my still being single. She enclosed her picture and wrote, "I'll marry you if nobody else will!"

Many of the letters I receive are from single people who ask my advice on how to be single and happy. I am moved by these letters because often they are filled with loneliness and sadness.

I am well acquainted with loneliness, but I don't think it's because I'm single.

I know of many married people who are lonely. Being married doesn't necessarily mean that loneliness will forever vanish. I have noticed people who are involved in other people, in helping others, in caring for others, in being concerned with others—these people aren't lonely.

Being single is an adventure. It's exciting. And so is being married. In the Bible Paul writes, " . . . I have learned how to get along happily whether I have much or little," and that is the attitude we need to develop if we are to know happiness at all in this life. Fame won't solve our problems, nor will marriage, money, or friends. These things may contribute to happiness, but true happiness can be found only in the Lord.

Chapter Thirty-Two

In 1975 another dream of mine came true. Billy Graham invited me to sing for a crusade in San Diego. I stood before 25,000 people and sang the words of my heart, "In the Image of God." It was a dramatic experience to stand backstage before the crusade began and pray with Dr. Graham and the others on the Graham team. He has built one of the most extensive and far-reaching ministries the world has ever known because of two facts: he loves Jesus and he loves people.

I have met great men and women in my life, people like Rex Humbard, who has a twinkle in his eye for all people he meets, and who lives each day to be of help to others. His love of God is unmistakably radiant, not only when he is on stage at the beautiful Cathedral of Tomorrow in Akron, Ohio, but also in a casual dinner situation, where I first met him.

Men like Pat Boone, Johnny Cash, George Otis, and Robert Schuller live lives exemplifying the Person of Jesus Christ. Many of the heroes I grew up admiring appealed to my sense of fantasy and adventure, but these men influenced the life of my soul and spirit.

In the summer of that year, Lawrence and I were invited to be in a Fourth of July parade in Dickinson, North Dakota. I was really honored to be in the same parade with him.

We closed our engagement at Harrah's, slept for approximately one hour, then drove from Lake Tahoe to Reno, where we boarded a plane to Bismarck. From there we took a private plane to Dickinson.

En route, somewhere, our baggage was lost—not an uncommon occurrence.

It was hectic because we were to appear in the Dickinson parade and then drive thirty miles to Medora, where we were to appear in another parade and celebration. Then, in addition, we had a performance that night.

You would think a schedule like this, with only an hour's sleep, would tire a man seventy-three years old, but not Lawrence. He seemed to thrive on it. He wasn't even ruffled over the missing luggage.

I sat next to him in the parade convertible, with the hot sun beating down upon us, and marveled. Back in Chicago when I was five or six years old I had seen Hopalong Cassidy in a parade and I remembered how impressed I had been.

It had been a thrill to actually see Hopalong Cassidy in person—there he was, for real, not a pic-

Sitting with North Dakota's Governor Link and his wife.
Behind us are Harold and Sheila Schafer and Lawrence.

ture or a movie, but the real person. And he was right there where I could almost reach out and touch him. He was waving his arm, moving his head, smiling and being alive right in front of me. I remembered how he looked directly at me—right at me. "Hoppy" looked at *me!* I was ecstatic. I felt that I was a hero, a great person.

The float in front of us, carrying Victor Julian and His Little Stars, paused. I looked over at Lawrence, who was waving both his arms and grinning at the people. I saw the crowds waving hats and handkerchiefs, grinning back at him, reaching for the car. I looked directly into the wide eyes

221

of children and felt wholly and suddenly awed.

I had never felt truly worthy of recognition; in fact, it surprised me when people paid attention to me. In high school I didn't feel I deserved to be senior class president; in the army I didn't feel worthy of the Spirit of Honor Medal; and certainly now, with the hands reaching out to the car, the shouts of praise filling the air, I didn't feel worthy. I watched Lawrence, who seemed right at home amid the clamor and attention, and I said, "Mr. Welk, how do you do it?"

He turned to me and said simply, "Tom, if you like the people, they'll like you right back."

I thought of the Schafers, of their success and the Glass Wax empire; yet they lived simple lives doing good for people. I thought of my own life and prayed again that it would count for something.

Early one morning I drove into the CBS parking lot for rehearsal. This particular morning I was early and had time to spare. Most mornings I would be rushing to be on time. (Being early is not one of my dominant virtues.) I thought maybe I'd stroll around the nearby Farmer's Market before going inside for rehearsal. But as I pulled my car around a corner, I saw a man. An old man, bent over, dressed in rags. His head was bowed and he shuffled along so slowly and pitifully, I thought he might be in pain.

I passed him, continuing on my way, but something in me had gone out to the man. I shifted gears and turned the car around. That man could be any one of us, someone's son, someone's grandfather . . . I had money in my wallet, a good job—certainly I had plenty to give.

I remembered my dream of carrying the old woman to get help. Turning off the ignition, I hurried across the lot to find the old man.

He had disappeared. I walked up and down the rows of cars, out onto the street, crossed to the edge of Farmer's Market, but to no avail.

Walking back to the studios now shining in the morning sun, I prayed, "Lord, give me opportunities to be helpful. And Lord, help that man I couldn't help."

In the summer of 1976 I was appearing at the Minnesota State Fair with the Lawrence Welk Show. It was hot and humid, and we had just finished our afternoon performance. The stage was quiet except for a group of men talking with Lawrence. I was passing by on the way to my dressing room when one of the men stepped out of the crowd and called to me. I recognized the voice immediately.

"Tom! Tom Netherton!" he called. It was Hubert Humphrey.

In the heat of the day, when most people are wrinkled and sweating, he looked fresh and immaculately groomed. "Come here, my boy," he said in a voice I had heard since my childhood.

"I just have to tell you how proud all of us in Minnesota are of you."

My chin dropped onto my sweaty collar.

"We watch the show all the time and every time you come on the screen, we applaud and say, 'That's our Tom from Minnesota!' "

I was sure I had never met a man so gracious. "We think you're doing a fantastic job, Tom, and you are a great representative of our state of Minnesota."

Then Muriel Humphrey, who had been swallowed up in the group of people, suddenly emerged and gave me a big hug. Without any prompting from her husband, she said, "Tom, we are all just so proud of you—all of us in Minnesota!"

A man like Hubert Humphrey had a way of making people feel important just by being near him.

Another man who makes people feel good about themselves is Dr. Robert Schuller, and when Dr. Schuller invited me to appear on his Sunday morning television broadcast, "The Hour of Power," I accepted immediately. Mom had written to him and told him he ought to have me on the program. (He thought it was such a touching gesture for her to write him that he responded by following her advice.) He told his television audiences about Mom's letter, and I laughed along with him, secretly thankful she hadn't told him some personal gem like how, at the age of six, I detested lima beans!

In 1977 I moved into the new three-story English Tudor style home I had built. I wandered through the rooms, examining the woodwork and floors, and thought about the future. I stepped out onto the terrace and looked across at the green California hills. My schedule for the coming month was a full one. There was an interview with *Inspiration* magazine, photographic sessions, meetings with my manager and landscaper; I also had meetings

My home in California, 1978.

with writer Marie Chapian, about writing this book.

I looked at my watch and knew I had to call the decorator about the dining room wallpaper, and then I had to dress for my dinner date. I took a breath and said out loud, "This is your house, Lord. I don't live here alone. I live here with you."

God had a plan for my life. I was certain of it, and I knew it was the morning of my life.

Chapter Thirty-Three

In 1978 I recorded two albums, *The Lord's Prayer* and *Love Songs,* on the Ranwood Label and was busy flying back and forth to Nashville, working on my next religious album, *The Hem of His Garment,* for Word Records.

One night a few of us sat talking over the music in my suite at Spence Manor across from the Country Music Hall of Fame. One of the musicians asked me, "Doesn't it seem odd to you to record an album of romantic love songs and then a religious album like this one?"

I smiled and looked him in the eye and said, "Who could better sing love songs than a person who knows the Source of love?"

We had finished the rhythm tracks and were now adding the strings and rest of the orchestra. I was pleased with this album. So were Bergen White, the arranger, and the others who worked on it. Bergen told me, "This is your best one yet, Tom. Your voice gets better every year."

I'm always pleased when I receive compliments from people I respect, and so I was happy to hear my voice was sounding good to trained and professional ears like Bergen's.

We finished the work on the album and I thanked God for the comparative ease with which it was produced. I had heard how the Beach Boys spent ninety hours in a studio to produce a single 45 rpm. disk back in 1966. The Beatles' *Sgt. Pepper's Lonely Hearts Club Band* took four months to produce. Often cutting a record in the past had been tedious and time-consuming, with the writing being done right there on the spot in the studio. We felt pleased our recording had gone smoothly and we were happy with the results.

I went home after the recording for a family reunion. Julie and her husband, Bruce, bubbled with news about their singing group, The Sixth Day. Brad and his wife, Jennifer, proudly showed little Amy's new tooth; Wendy had a new job and a new boyfriend; and Mom was fluttering over each of us with love and talk of us all living closer one day. She recounted the story of how Brad got mad at me once when we were young, threw a pen quill at me, and how hilarious I looked with it sticking out of my head.

"That's probably when your hair got real blond," Julie snickered.

I enjoyed being with the family like this. I loved them all, and because my times with them were so few, I appreciated these moments even more.

We showed home movies of the family in Fort Bragg, Fort Benning, Fort Riley, Palos Heights; and we roared with laughter at each reel. There

Top: *Playing with my niece Amy, daughter of my brother Brad and his wife Jennifer. Isn't she cute?* Bottom left: **My sister Wendy.** Bottom right: **My sister Julie.**

Top: *My mom, Lillian Netherton.* Bottom: *Backstage with (l. to r.) my sister Wendy, my brother Brad, his wife Jennifer, and my sister Julie.*

was usually more of Dad's eye blinking, not realizing he was being filmed as he figured out how to set the camera. Then I put a reel on the projector that shocked us all into silence. My grandpa's face suddenly appeared on the screen.

"Dad!" Brad whispered. He was looking at us from the little screen and smiling. Then he turned and drew Grandma into the picture. She waved her hand at us and smiled, too. They both just stood there flickering in the faded light of the film, smiling. Grandpa's mouth moved and he was saying something. They stayed that way, smiling at us in a white pool of light from another time and place. Then they laughed and Grandpa said something again; they waved once more and the film began to sputter on the reel, clicking their faces off the screen.

We were quiet and then Julie asked, "What do you suppose Dad was saying?"

"Maybe he said the light was too bright," Wendy answered.

"No, I don't think so," Mom said. "I think he was saying what I feel tonight, and that is, happy and proud of my Little Ones."

"I think so, too," I said quietly. Seeing his beloved face on the little movie screen shook me more than I cared to admit. I would long carry with me the memory of him smiling and waving at me from some other white distant place.

There were many pressures and obligations to meet. I left Minnesota for another appearance on the "700 Club" in Portsmouth, Virginia, and then on to the "PTL Club" in Charlotte, North Carolina. I was now headlining special events around the country like the Azalea Festival in Charlotte, North Carolina, the Star Series in Lee High Acres, Florida, the Edison Pageant of Light in Fort Myers, Florida, and the March of Dimes Program in Long Beach, California, with Carol Lawrence and B. J. Thomas. I even co-hosted the Little Junior Miss Beauty Pageant in Baton Rouge, Louisiana.

I was delighted when the Van Wezel Performing Arts Center in Sarasota, Florida, invited me to headline there. I had appeared there once before as Anita Bryant's opening act, and now I would be the headliner with Vonda Kay Van Dyke as my opening act.

With all these performances, the standing ovations, the reviews saying things like, "Tom Netherton's show is the best of the season," and "Tom Netherton looks like a Greek god with a rich baritone voice like you used to hear in Broadway," and Tom Netherton is ". . . a first-rate singer with looks even Robert Redford would envy," I began to get a little puffed up.

In fact, I began to feel restless and started to mope around the studio, feeling dissatisfied with some of the numbers I was given to sing on the Welk Show. I wanted to sing from the heart. I wanted to be me. After all, I was now accustomed to performing for two hours alone doing my razzle-em, dazzle-em—I was, as one reporter said, "a dashing voice who could be a major star. . . ."

One thing I hadn't learned yet is that a person mustn't believe his reviews and shouldn't ever believe all his publicity.

It was Johnny Zell who jumped in and saved me from myself.

"Pride, Tom, pride!" he said in a loving voice. "If God wants you to do your own thing on television, he will present the opportunity for you to pursue. Now pull yourself together and thank him that you are able to sing to 35 million people every week. And thank him that the Lawrence Welk Show makes it possible."

I knew he was right.

Sometimes I wonder where we would be if it weren't for other believers who pray and stand with us ready to help us when we're wrong. Just when I'm feeling the worst, God shows me his best.

I again went to the Lord and asked his forgiveness. I saw how I had been deceived in my thinking. I knew that pride was a killer. It had destroyed many a well-intentioned Christian. It could easily destroy a performer who depends so heavily on public response for his keep. I needed to get my priorities in order.

The Lord proved to me later that he had a sense of humor when one reviewer wrote that he didn't like my show at all. My first reaction was to feel angry and slighted. Then I remembered if I'm not going to get puffed up and proud over the good reviews, I shouldn't get discouraged over the bad ones, either.

I needed to remember it was God's approval I lived for, no one else's.

Chapter
Thirty-Four

Liking yourself isn't the easiest thing in the world to do. I've met scores of people who have lived out most of their lives not really liking themselves at all. You'd be surprised at the number of television and movie stars who are adored by millions, but whose lives are filled with and even motivated by self-hate.

Every week I receive letters from men, women, and young people from all over America who ask me questions about self-acceptance.

When I was a little boy I dreamed about being someone else. I had heroes. I imitated and hoped I'd be worthwhile one day like my heroes were. Now I believed with my whole heart that knowing I am important to God, precious in his sight, I am a totally acceptable person. I could accept my failures and my successes, my good points and my bad.

In show business it's easy to become a victim of other people's opinions and life styles, but this problem exists in other professions, as well. There are housewives who are victims of their neighbors' opinions, students who act according to what their friends think, businessmen who are always trying to keep one step ahead of their competitors and dying early because of it.

I see this attitude prevailing in the church, too. I visit many churches every year and I am always amazed when I look around and see a whole sanctuary filled with people who look alike, act alike, talk alike, and even pray alike.

The most familiar prayer I hear is what I call the King James-type prayer. A person will be happily chatting in normal speech patterns using familiar colloquialisms and metaphors, but then when it comes time to pray, he stiffens, his voice changes, and he speaks with a new set of usage rules. A child has to be trained to speak King James. Why the switch?

Maybe it's because the pastor prays that way from the pulpit or somebody else prays that way. But really, I wonder, what's wrong with talking to God in the same way we speak in everyday life? It may be that some people have a strong desire to hold on to tradition. It also may be that speaking in King James English to the Lord is a show of respect. I personally believe that we show our respect to the Lord by our love and our actions toward him. Formalized, stiff prayers aren't necessarily signs of respect. Often they are a sign of noncommitment.

I believe God likes me just the way I am and that's why I can learn to like me just the way I am. I believe he likes hearing from me regardless of whether I know how to pray in King James or not.

He doesn't want us to be robots. He created us, each one of us, perfectly and uniquely individual. I'm glad for that.

I'm glad I'm who I am. But it's easy to fall into the trap of basing my opinions of myself on what other people think about me. It's easy to lose sight of the fact that self-worth does not rely upon somebody else's opinion.

Even though I tend to be a loner, the Lord is working on me, showing me to trust people. I am learning to allow people into my life without worrying that they'll clutter it up or bring confusion and hurt.

I have a quote on my datebook. It says:

> *Everyone in the world has a burden.*
> *It's not the burden that counts,*
> *but how you carry it.*

Maybe the reason I chose the entertainment business is to live out the dream to play-act someone else. But I've decided my own life is a good life. And furthermore, I've decided to be glad to be me.

Every one of us should be able to say that. It's a matter of teaching ourselves to think these thoughts and say these words about ourselves. Instead of thinking negatives, we choose to think true thoughts.

When I was a young boy I wished I weren't always

taller than everybody else. I could never be incon-spicuous because I was always a foot taller than the rest of the world.

Really, when I think of it, there are probably a hundred things about me I wish I could change, and maybe that's true in your life, too. But it's our way of thinking that needs changing. We need to start thanking God for making us just the way we are. God didn't create us with negative attitudes. We develop them on our own, but we can change them, too.

When I decided to cut my hair short, I was going on vacation to Hawaii. I liked the casual look of the hair style. But when I appeared on television again, the audience had quite a different opinion.

"How *could* you do that to your hair, Tom?"

"You look awful!"

"You're not half as handsome now. Let your hair grow back the way it was before."

In answer, all I could say was, "But I like it." (Besides, it was the first time I had seen my ears for a long time!)

Occasionally someone will say, "You people on the Lawrence Welk Show don't look real. You look too good to be true."

I usually answer, "We are supposed to look good." Some of us may appear as though we have no problems and life for us is just a dream and a song. The reason for this is, the show is geared to lift people up; to take us all away from everyday hassles and problems. Lawrence feels it's refresh-ing to see wholesome, happy people singing good music with a simple format. It looks like millions of viewers have agreed with him for years as each week the cast of the Lawrence Welk Show arrives in their living rooms making music, singing, and smiling, and having a good time.

The girls on the show tease me that if our viewers could see me asleep on the airplane, my suave romantic image would be finished forever. "Tom, did you know you sleep with your mouth open?" Ava teased me one day as we were coming in for a landing at the Omaha airport.

"I do not."

"You sure do, brother, and I'll prove it to you."

She produced a Polaroid snapshot of me sound asleep in the seat with my head against the window and my mouth hanging wide open.

Whenever things get a little dull, she pulls out that picture. It's always good for a big laugh.

The cast members tease each other continually. Often I am paired with pretty red-haired Sandi Griffiths, who sings in the trio with Mary Lou and Gail. Sandi is the tallest girl. As we are twirling around on the stage together in a waltz, she'll say sweetly, "Gee, Tom, you dance just terribly." I'll answer, "Why, thank you, Sandi. Tell me, what did you do to your hair tonight?"

"Oh, do you like it?"

"It's a disaster."

Even though we joke with each other, we are quite supportive of one another's careers. We stand offstage and watch each other perform and will always boast how terrific the other person is.

At Lake Tahoe every year nearly a thousand people pack into the South Shore Room at Harrah's twice a night to see the Lawrence Welk Show. The audiences love the show because it's clean, positive, wholesome, and everybody has a good time. Lawrence always enjoys his audiences and cavorts around on the stage with limitless energy. He is proud of his age. (And when his birthday gets near, he loves to have the audiences sing "happy birthday" to him.)

One night at Lake Tahoe, Mr. and Mrs. Eddie Shipstad of Ice Follies fame came backstage. They are lovely and tender-hearted people whom I liked immediately.

"You know, Tom, one thing we've never compromised is our belief in a good, clean show," Mrs. Shipstad said, with her eyes twinkling.

"Our shows are family type shows. If you can't take the kiddies to it, we won't do it."

They told me they believed in clean entertainment no matter what the rest of the entertainment world was doing. "We stand for everything good and so does Lawrence," Mrs. Shipstad said, taking my arm.

"Tom, you are an inspiration to many people. Don't ever compromise."

I value advice from a wise woman like Lu Shipstad.

If we don't like ourselves just the way we are, then we can easily be pressured into compromising our values and our morals.

Chapter
Thirty-Five

I believe in America. In my act I often do a patriotic medley that at first I worried about. I wasn't sure how it would go over. I wear a red, white, and blue costume with stars and stripes and hundreds of sparkling mirrors and rhinestones all over the pants and jacket. (I tell people I bought it at Evel Knievel's garage sale.)

I sing about our country from a grateful heart. I wonder if my own personal success story could happen in any other country but ours.

Often I'll include a religious number in my act. One of my conductors was aghast at the idea. "Man, that is far out!"

"It'll work, you'll see."

"I'll have to see it to believe it."

People have been singing Gospel outside the church for years and years. People like the Clara Ward Singers, the Staple Singers, Edwin Hawkins Singers, James Cleveland, Ethel Waters, Mahalia

Jackson; moderns like Johnny Cash, Pat Boone, and the late Elvis (who often got on his knees in concert and sang "Precious Lord, Take My Hand").

The first time I sang "How Great Thou Art" to a secular audience with just a piano as background, the audience looked as though they were in suspended animation. Nobody moved. Then when I finished the number, the place broke into a tumult of applause. They clapped wildly, cheered, stood to their feet, and applauded until they sat back down, almost as exhausted as I.

As a little boy back in Fort Riley I wondered if church was for sissies. Now I saw God was no sissy. Nothing intimidated him. Certainly not a show business atmosphere in which there were so many men and women needing answers in their lives.

When I added the patriotic medley, the response took me by surprise. The first time I performed it, people rose to their feet and cheered.

I had been concerned about my costume and I asked Norma Zimmer, who was also singing at the concert with the Birmingham Symphony Orchestra, whether she thought I should wear the flashy costume or not. Her bright eyes twinkled as she said, "Of course, Tom, wear it! People love colorful things and your costume is in good taste!" I admired Norma because she was sophisticated and yet unaffected and full of fun. She is an inspiration to me and to everyone on the Lawrence Welk Show. I'm grateful she's my friend.

I took her advice, and walked out on stage in my outrageous costume in the concert with the Birmingham Symphony Orchestra. The audience

Norma Zimmer, a beautiful lady and wonderful friend.

went nuts. They whistled and clapped and carried on quite unlike a symphony orchestra audience. I discovered there are a lot of people who are very patriotic! I am not alone in my love and appreciation of my country.

I travel across the country, staying in motels and hotels in various cities, and I meet friendly, wonderful Americans everywhere. I don't believe in downgrading America or the American system. So often I'll hear someone say, "Oh, America is going to pieces. America is full of corruption." Especially since Watergate, the American people have felt disillusioned and dismayed about things. But I believe we ought to pray for our country, not condemn it.

When I was in New York for an engagement at the Waldorf Astoria, I took long walks around the city. New York is not a typical American city, just as Mexico City is not typical of Mexico as a whole. Over 10 million people live in this great city and I loved walking among the crowds, looking in shops, and playing the part of the tourist. New York, like Los Angeles, seems separate from the rest of the country. It's hard to find similarities between the folks who run the dry goods store in Saginaw, Michigan, and the clerks at Joseph Magnim or Eric Ross in Los Angeles. And eating in a restaurant in Madison, Wisconsin, or Uniontown, Pennsylvania, is as similar to eating in a deli or restaurant in New York as the sheriff of Mayberry is similar to a New York riot squad.

One day I was standing in Times Square when a garbage truck passed me. Then it stopped suddenly in front of me a ways. When I drew closer, a man in dirty overalls, hanging on the back of the truck, yelled in a heavy Bronx accent, "Hey! Aren't you Tom Netherton from the Lawrence Welk Show?"

I waved back at the man. "Yes, I am! Hi!"

"Hey! Listen! Tell Lawrence all the gah-bage men in New York say hello!"

"I'll do that!"

"And listen! You're a terrific singer! Keep it up!"

If they had asked me to sing "Melancholy Baby" right there on the sidewalk, I probably would have. They waved and grinned, and the truck grunted off down Broadway and disappeared around the corner.

Big cities have a tendency to swallow a person,

but they are also invigorating with a special energy and pulse that cannot be found elsewhere. I am not always recognized on the street, as in the experience with the New York garbage collectors. Many times I go unrecognized even after giving my name.

One morning I sat in the busy waiting room of an advertising agency in Los Angeles, thumbing through a copy of *People* magazine and thinking of postcards I needed to have printed, when I overheard the receptionist saying to herself, "Work. I hate it."

I smiled at her. "Were you talking to me?"

"No. Just talking to myself. This place does that to me. I start talking to myself."

"I do it, too."

"Yeah? Well, I should have been a plumber."

"What makes you say that?"

"I mean, I should have been a ditch digger, a lion tamer, a sword swallower! Anything but a typist-receptionist."

"But why?"

"Ha! Don't ask. Nobody appreciates me. I could drop dead already and nobody would care."

I took a breath and told her about Someone who did appreciate her.

"I never would have thought of such a thing," she said, her voice faltering.

"I'm serious. I'm an entertainer and every time I do a show, I know Jesus is sitting front row center. And I know he *enjoys* what I do."

"Incredible!"

"I know he is listening and enjoying every minute."

"Unbelievable!"

She fumbled with a note pad, tapped a pencil, and stared at the rows of buttons on the telephone.

"Would you believe it? This is the longest time these phones have been quiet since I've worked here." Then she raised her eyes to me. "I have to tell you that what you are telling me is the most incredible thing I have ever heard."

"It is also true."

"That knocks me out. Just knocks me out. Jesus sits front row center—"

She leaned forward. "Do you think he cares about everybody that way? I mean, how about people like—"

"Like you?"

"Yeah."

We talked for an hour. The telephones actually didn't ring once. (She insisted it was a miracle already.) When I went inside for my appointment, I hoped she knew in a very real sense that she was important and that Jesus was right there with her as she answered telephones, typed, and did her job.

As I prepared to leave the agency that day, I was delighted with everything: life, God, me, everything. Then the receptionist, smiling cheerfully, waved at me and called, "By the way, *Don*, where *are* you appearing?"

Chapter
Thirty-Six

I dislike clutter and disorganization. Maybe it's a carry-over from my army days, but I am basically a neat person. I'm not the type to allow dishes to stack up in the sink or to leave clothes piled in heaps on the floor. I try to be organized in my business affairs, too. Often it surprises people because I think I appear to be the naive, youthful type.

"Here, Tom, sign this."

"No."

"But it's important!"

"I'll take it home and read it first. If I decide it's agreeable, then I'll sign."

"But it's urgent!"

"I'll decide that."

I probably spend more time than most entertainers do, going over business arrangements and making decisions that ordinarily are handled by other people. It may be the characteristic in me that never enjoyed team sports, the part of me that doesn't like gambling—that part of me that finds little pleasure in "chance." I like to be in control of my life.

But sometimes crazy things happen and I find myself smack in the middle of some chaotic circumstances over which I have no control whatsoever.

An experience in Lincoln, Illinois, at the Lincoln County Fair, is a good example. All my neatness went right down the drain. Literally!

It was a cloudy day and 3,500 people sat in the outdoor stands to see the show. Everything was going along smoothly. The warm-up act was out on stage and I was standing in the wings waiting to go on. Partially through their act it began to drizzle. By the time they had finished, it was raining steadily. The manager came puffing up to me. "Tom, can you go on? If you can go on for just twenty minutes, we won't have to give the people their money back. You're the star of the show. They came to see you. What do you say, Tom?"

I looked at the outdoor open stage, now under an unremitting downpour. My white suit with rhinestones and embroidered work, white shirt, and white shoes would get ruined out there. I laughed and told the manager, "Of course, I'll go on."

I remembered the Medora Musical where actors, musicians, horses, dogs, wagons, and elaborate sets were practically flooded on the stage. Yet the show went on and everybody had a great time.

The people were holding newspapers and umbrellas over their heads, and when I walked out on the wet stage in the rain, they cheered. I assumed they'd be surging up the aisles to get out of the rain, but nobody was leaving. I sang my opening number, "I'm gonna love you like nobody's loved you, come rain or come shine—"

I knew it was going to be fun after that one, so I followed it with "Once Upon a Time" and then "You Are the Sunshine of My Life."

By this time everybody was soaked through to the skin, including me, but we were having fun. My makeup was running off my face, my hair dripped over my eyes, and there was mud and water everywhere I stepped as I sang "On a Clear Day."

Twenty minutes passed, and so did another twenty minutes. I thought if all these people were willing to stay outside in the rain, I wouldn't disappoint them. It was thundering by the time I sang "You Are My Sunshine," and I could hardly see the front row of people through the rain.

I didn't want to do a performance without being able to see the people, so I did the show from the audience, moving among the people. I always have fun chatting with the audiences, but today, with the rain splashing down on us, we had a great time of it. When I finished the show with "How Great Thou Art," the people gave a standing ovation.

I looked half drowned when I sloshed off stage. The manager shook his head in genuine appreciation. "You know, I've seen very few performers go out in the rain like that," he told me. "And what's more, I've never seen so many people stay for a whole show in the rain!"

When I got a glimpse of myself in the mirror in the dressing room, I couldn't help but laugh. I was muddy, soaked, and my sparkling white costume with the rhinestones was now dripping and sagging like old paint peeling off a barn.

I thought of the audience—3,500 people who had to be almost as wet as I was. I hoped it was worth it for them. It certainly was for me.

I laughed at the bedraggled reflection in the mirror. "So you think you're Mr. *Neat*, huh?"

Being on the road so much of the time, many things can go wrong. I arrived in Yakima, Washington, on a beautiful May afternoon for an evening church concert. When I went to pick up my luggage, I discovered it hadn't arrived. It didn't arrive by the time the concert was to begin, either, so I went on stage in a blue velvet suit and sneakers.

In Tarrant, Alabama, at one of my concerts, I asked the audience if they had any questions they'd like to ask me. One little girl raised her hand and asked, "Do yoll like pats?"

"I'm sorry, I didn't hear—?"

"Ah said, do yoll like pats?"

My smile stuck in place, "Pats?"

"Ycs, pats. Pats! Pats!"

I was confused. Then someone else in the audience shouted, "Pets! Do yoll like *pets*?"

The audience burst into laughter. I laughed, too, at my own ignorance, but then I remembered a brown-eyed, long-nosed face next to mine, with mouth open and tongue licking the side of my face. I remembered her long-haired coat and her smells and I remembered her death when she was thirteen years old.

"Yes," I said to the still giggling girl. "I sure do like pets. My favorite was a dog named Lassie. She lived for thirteen years, and when she died, I lost a good friend."

There were other questions, but I was remembering our brave and noble dog, Lassie. I remembered Mom bringing her into the vet's office when she was dying. They arrived at the office and Lassie lay on the floor of the waiting room unmoving. Mom called, "Come, Lassie," and the dog rose on very unsteady legs and followed her into the office.

When the vet lifted the dog onto the examining table, he shook his head. "Mrs. Netherton, I'm sorry. This dog is dead."

"But she just walked in here!"

"I tell you, this was one obedient dog. I think she was dead before she walked through that door. But you called her and she obeyed."

Funny how a person remembers things. . . .

Early in 1978 when I was working on the plans for my swimming pool, I glanced over at the stack of letters that had arrived that morning. I smiled as I thought of the invitations from several girls to escort them to their proms, the inquiries why I wasn't married yet, and questions like, "If I sent you cookies, would you eat them?"

I received letters from young people who shared their problems and burdens with me and many hours would be spent answering each letter individually.

"Doesn't anything ever go wrong for you?" one letter read. "Do you ever have problems like I do?"

My biggest problem at the moment was finishing work on the pool plans so I could be ready to pick up my date by six o'clock. It wasn't often I had a free evening and I was going to enjoy every minute of this one.

My date was a girl friend from my Bible school days. We would have a candlelight dinner at Castaway's, a Polynesian restaurant. I felt comfortable with Joni. She was fun to be with and I could talk to her.

"I think it's odd that people think you haven't got a problem in the world," she told me over the appetizer. "They don't realize the pressure and strain an entertainer is under all the time. I do, because I know you."

"I'm glad you know me, Joni," I said.

She smiled. "Do your fans think you're perfect?"

"Some do."

"Well, Mr. Perfect, I've got news for them. Your shirt is buttoned wrong."

While we were sitting outside on the patio underneath the flickering light of the Polynesian torches, I put my arm around her and whispered in her ear, "I've got prom proposals from dozens of gorgeous young women in my pocket."

"And you've also got a parking ticket on your car," she whispered back, glancing over my shoulder and seeing my 280Z parked in front of a driveway.

I've tended to be a loner, but I don't think loners are happy people. I think it's sad not to need and want other people. When it came to crowds, such as party situations or large gatherings, I could be the life of the party: outgoing, witty, chatting with everybody and having a very nice time. But when it came to relationships that demanded commitment and consistency, I found myself on the short end of the stick.

Maybe that is because growing up I was alone so much of the time; and I have found it safer that way. But people who don't reach out to other people aren't happy. I was learning that.

A couple of weeks later, when I was performing in Florida, I called off a party I was invited to and told my date, Ginger, "I'd really rather not go to the party, even though it looks as if it would be a lot of fun."

"It's OK with me, Tom."

"I'd rather get to know you better. Let's just go somewhere and talk. You and I alone."

The girls I most enjoy dating are Christian girls who share my beliefs. We can laugh and be funny, talk and be serious, and know that we belong to the Lord. He is our common interest.

And I won't lead a girl on, trying to make her think she's more important to me than she actually is. I date several girls and don't hide the fact. But when I fall in love for keeps, I'll be as faithful as the dawn every morning.

Chapter
Thirty-Seven

I t was late afternoon and I could hear the sounds of rush hour traffic outside as I sat in Di'Fabrizio's custom shoe store in Los Angeles. I remembered how, not so long ago, I had been *selling* shoes, and not custom-made ones, either.

Now here I sat, smug as a cat, while a man measured my feet for a pair of stage shoes that would cost $300 a pair. I looked on the shelf and saw names on boxes of shoes, people whose shoes Di'Fabrizio made: Perry Como, Dinah Shore, James Mason, Frankie Avalon, Burt Reynolds, Zsa Zsa Gabor, Tom Jones. My feet were in good company. I wondered if they were any happier than they used to be when I had put them into cheap sneakers and sweat socks.

Pat Boone had given me the name of his tailor in Beverly Hills, so now I was wearing clothes stars wore.

Actually, my favorite clothes are dungarees, loose-fitting shirts and sneakers, or preferably bare feet.

I was learning a lot about stars, and not only about the clothes they wore and who their tailors and shoemakers were.

I went to Las Vegas to see Bobby Vinton's show. His road show conductor, Joe Parnello, was also my conductor. When Bobby learned I was in the audience, he said from the stage, "Ladies and gentlemen, I want you to meet a very special person who is in our audience tonight. I know you all know and love him from the Lawrence Welk Show—Mr. Tom Netherton!"

The spotlight fell on me and I rose to my feet and bowed. I was amazed at such a warm and generous gesture on the part of a star of his caliber. He invited me backstage after the show, and he and his wife took me to dinner. Then they had me stay for the second show and they also paid my tab.

I was beginning to discover the genuine friendliness and kindness of people who are tops in the business. People like Carol Burnett, who was so gracious when she met me that you would have thought I was a long lost cousin.

And Sammy Davis, Jr., joked, "You see this guy here, you look at him—you see he's good looking, talented and *tall.* — You know what I'm going to do to him? I'm going to sock him right in the knee!"

People like Eddie Arnold, Danny Thomas, Liberace, and Jim Nabors have been so nice to all of us on the Lawrence Welk Show. They have come backstage after performances and lavished praise on all the performers and musicians. It didn't take long for me to see that the greater the star, the more gracious he or she can be.

In 1978 I performed with Carol Lawrence and B. J. Thomas at the March of Dimes Benefit in Long Beach, California, with the Long Beach Symphony. I found working with them a delight. They are strong Christians and beautiful people.

And it's always a real joy to work with Dale Evans Rogers in concert. She is a dynamic example of the power of Christ in a life—plus she's just "down home folks" and I love her.

With my heavy travel schedule, it is a blessing to have travel agents like Sandy and Ron Benson, who own the Skyline Travel Agency in Los Angeles. They've become good friends. Sandy worries that I don't eat properly, with all the restaurant meals I eat, so she often brings me dishes of her delicious home cooking. The Bensons have done so many kind things and gone out of their way so often for me that they are not only the best travel agents in the whole world, but wonderful friends as well.

I enjoy making new friends in my travels. When I took my vacation to the Caribbean one year, I had the opportunity to spend some time with a married couple I met on the Island of St. Thomas.

I sat in the coffee shop of my hotel having lunch served by tanned, friendly waitresses in starched cotton uniforms. I started talking to a middle-aged couple sitting near me. They seemed to be a happy couple who had known several years of marriage and contentment together.

The following day, however, I saw the wife

walking alone along the beach not far from my hotel room.

"Could I talk to you for a few minutes?" she asked when she spotted me.

"Sure, come on, let's walk."

So we walked together past the thatched cabanas and she told me something which surprised me.

"I'm thinking of leaving my husband."

"Leaving him? But why?"

"I just don't see any other way."

She told me she was married to "an impossible man," a man who didn't care about anything in this world except himself. She was tired of being his servant and slave and wanted out.

I had heard these complaints before.

"Trouble is," I told her, "you're looking at the *problem.*"

She gave me a quizzical glance.

"It's true. You're seeing the problem and not the solution. What would happen if you changed your way of thinking and saw him as being the kind of husband you want?"

"I don't know. . . ."

"Are you a praying person?"

"Well, I was confirmed. I've been to church, but I'm not—well, I'm not the religious type."

"Neither am I."

"Oh?"

"I'm the *believing* type. There's a difference. And I believe in solutions. I believe God can work miracles in lives and that he can change people."

"My husband will never change."

"He won't if you keep believing that way."

We walked and talked in the shadows of the palm trees and wound our way back toward the hotel pool.

"Well, how about it?" I asked her, looking her right in the eye. "Would you like to change your defeatist attitude? Would you like to believe God? He'll not only change your husband, he'll change *you*."

"I think I need that."

She prayed with me and I felt a rush of hope for this couple. I knew God was in the business of restoring marriages because he was in the business of restoring lives.

She laughed as we parted. "You know, it seems odd. Here you are, single—and you're giving marriage counseling."

"Well, I'd like to be married. I just haven't found the right girl yet."

"I think if I had your life, Tom, I'd be really happy."

"Ah, yes, I receive many letters from people who tell me that. Ridiculous. The grass always looks greener on the other side of the hill. And it isn't. There are problems in everyone's lives."

She smiled and nodded her head.

"But with Christ in my life, it makes everything worthwhile."

"He will be in *my* life from now on, too."

"Thank God."

"Yes, Tom. I do thank God."

She ran down the hill to the pool, and I watched her as she joined her husband, who was sunning on a pool chair. She turned and waved to me and, as I headed back to my room, I saw her kiss the top of his head.

"Yes," I thought. "Thank God."

Chapter
Thirty-Eight

I pulled into the parking lot at the Van Wezel Performing Arts Center in Sarasota and lost my breath at the sight before me. There were cars as far as I could see, and crowds of people going into the beautiful bayfront auditorium. I swallowed and sat very still, looking at the sight before me. "Lord, there is only one event going on in there today, one show—that show is the Tom Netherton Show. Dear Lord, these people are here to see *me.*"

It doesn't seem possible. All these people to see me!

"Lord, touch these people today, touch them in some way through me. Let me bring something good into their lives today."

Just then a traffic policeman tapped on my window. "Can't park there, fella," he said. "You'll have to pull up." I waved and started the engine.

A group of teen-age girls was crossing the parking lot in front of my car. They were talking and giggling, hurrying to the entrance ramp. They didn't notice me, but I sat watching them until they disappeared into the crowds entering the building.

I pulled my car into a parking space, reached into the back for my clothes bag, and grinned at the early afternoon sky.

An older couple walked past me, chatting to another couple behind them. I nodded to them and said, "Hello. How are you?"

I entered the stage entrance and found my dressing room. I thought of the many times at my Christian concerts people had said to me, "Oh, Tom, it's so wonderful that you sing Christian music and use your talents for the Lord."

I answer, "But I am always using my talents for the Lord. I don't have to be in a church to sing for Jesus." I sing amid the clink of dishes and supper club laughter and talk; I sing while waiters stack dirty dishes in the kitchen after the dinner hour; I sing at fairs outdoors while yards away 4-H cows await their fates and kids squeal on revolving ferris wheels. I sing in my car and I sing in my own backyard when there's nobody around but the crickets.

"But, Tom," I hear them say, "you're lucky! You've had all the right breaks." I realize I've been blessed by the Lord and I'm glad my career is in his hands. If he chose to move me on to something else tomorrow, ending my singing career, I'd still consider myself blessed. And I'd head toward new dawns with the same enthusiasm I felt now for entertaining.

I slipped my feet into my Di'Fabrizio boots and

remembered what my brother's wife, Jennifer, told me the last time I was with them. "At least you're not a prudish Christian, Tom," she had said. "Everywhere you go, you seem right at home."

She didn't realize what effect her words would have on me. I didn't want to be known as "religious" or "stuffy" or a prude. Jesus is none of those things. I didn't want to be known as just a performer, either.

I know God expects us to use our talents, but our talents alone aren't what make us successful people. We all have the choice to be either God-centered or self-centered. If the only strength we have is our own, then we are missing out on the power of God. We're missing the power that he wants to give us. There is a dynamic life for us to lead and it requires more than just our talents.

Talent doesn't make us right at home wherever we go. The person we are inside is what accomplishes that.

When Johnny Cash once asked country singer Sonny James how he managed to live a Christian life in the entertainment field, he answered simply, "I live it by *being* who I am. I am first a Christian. Then I am an entertainer."

Every believer ought to be able to say, whether we're entertainers, bricklayers, housewives, students, salespeople, officers in the armed forces, or waiters in a restaurant, we are first Christians.

The dressing room was quiet except for the low murmur of the air conditioner. There were 2,000 people filling the beautiful lavender auditorium.

From here I would be playing concerts all over the country, but for now I knew my attention had to be on the show I was about to perform. I changed into my black velvet jacket edged with fine glass beading, made a final check in the mirror and then left the dressing room. As I walked down the dark hallway toward the stage I heard the orchestra begin the overture. I waited off stage and adjusted my shirt cuffs as the announcer said, "Ladies and gentlemen, Mr. Tom Netherton!" I heard the applause and then stepped out from the darkness onto the stage as the spotlights spilled over me, warm and bright like the dawn of a new day. For me, it really was the morning of my life.